Honduras

A Country Guide

Honduras
A Country Guide

Tom Barry & Kent Norsworthy

The Inter-Hemispheric Education Resource Center

Albuquerque, New Mexico

Published by The Inter-Hemispheric Education Resource Center

ISBN: 0-911213-22-8

Library of Congress Catalog Card Number: 90-81481

The Inter-Hemispheric Education Resource Center
Box 4506 * Albuquerque, New Mexico * 87196

Acknowledgments

Honduras: A Country Guide, like the other books in this series, represents the contributions of numerous Resource Center staff members. For research assistance, we are grateful to Jenny Beatty, Joan MacLean, Felipe Montoya, Debra Preusch, and Thomas Weiss. Eric Shultz of the Honduras Information Center also helped with research. Connie Adler edited the book, and Jenny Beatty assisted with her proofreading, wordprocessing, and production skills. We are also grateful to Steve Sefton, Phil Shepherd, and Zenaida Velásquez for carefully reading and commenting on the manuscript.

Table of Contents

The Resource Center

The Inter-Hemispheric Education Resource Center is a private non-profit research and policy institute located in Albuquerque, New Mexico. Founded in 1979, the Resource Center produces books, policy reports, and audiovisuals about U.S. foreign relations with third world countries. Among its most popular materials are *The Central America Fact Book* and the quarterly *Bulletin* mailed to subscribers for $5 annually ($7.50 outside the United States). For a catalogue of publications, please write to: The Resource Center, Box 4506, Albuquerque, NM 87196.

Honduras

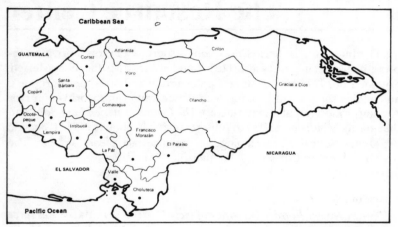

Inforpress Centroamericana

Introduction

Honduras, long relegated to the backwater of Central American politics and economy, was pushed and pulled forward in the 1980s into a new position of prominence. Suddenly, Hondurans found their country being hailed as an "oasis of peace," as a "model of democratization," and as "pivotal in U.S. policy toward Central America." Centrally located on the isthmus and bordering three countries experiencing violent political conflict, Honduras was selected by Washington as a stable platform for its interventionism in the region.

About the size of Ohio, Honduras is a largely mountainous country of 4.8 million. Honduras has access to two oceans — through the Gulf of Fonseca on the Pacific side and the Caribbean ports on the Atlantic side. Ethnically, the country is largely homogeneous — with over 90 percent of its citizens being *mestizo*.

Tegucigalpa, located in central Honduras, is the capital and also the country's largest city, but San Pedro Sula is the industrial center and most prosperous city. It is the business hub of the North Coast — which since the early 1900s has been the base of the country's most dynamic agricultural and agro-industrial production. The Caribbean departments of Cortés, Atlántida, and Colón stretch along the North Coast, with Puerto Cortés, Tela, La Ceiba, and Trujillo being the principal Caribbean ports. To the east lies the isolated department of Gracias a Dios, a frontier region inhabited mainly by Miskito Indians. The two other eastern border departments are Olancho, which has a deserved reputation for wild west lawlessness, and El Paraíso, which became the base of contra operations during the 1980s.

The dry and environmentally devastated department of Choluteca lies to the south and along the Gulf of Fonseca. In recent years, crop failures have contributed to the deepening poverty and hunger of the residents of Choluteca and the departments bordering El Salvador: Valle, La Paz, Intibucá, Lempira, and Ocotepeque. In central Honduras are the departments of Francisco Morazán (where Tegucigalpa is located), Comayagua, and Yoro. Farther west along the Guatemalan border are Santa Bárbara and Copán.

Like other Central American nations, Honduras is undergoing rapid urbanization. The arrival every month of 5,000 immigrants from rural areas has swelled the population of Tegucigalpa. Thirty years ago only 72,000 people lived in Tegucigalpa. Today the population is over a half million and will probably reach two million by the turn of the century if current migration and birth rates continue.

Oil paintings by local artists present an idyllic picture of rural Honduras: a storybook land of peace and tranquility lush with tropical colors and fruits, a world of red tile roofs, white churches, and cobblestone streets. Indeed, rural Honduras does seem a world apart from hectic urban life. But is a benighted world lacking the most basic of services— trapped by centuries of poverty and neglect, and cast off as hopelessly backward by the forces of modernization. What peace there is comes mostly from a stillness induced by unrelenting hunger and violated expectations.

Although in the geographical center of Central America, Honduras has had the reputation of being the exception to the region's history of brutal repression. Unlike neighboring states where class tensions and political disputes have been marked by violence, in Honduras compromise and smooth community relations have been favored over confrontation, peaceful solutions over bloodshed. This tradition was severely tested in the 1980s as Honduras was thrust into the regional turmoil. Wars raged across the border in three of its neighboring states—and in two of those conflicts Honduras took an active partisan role.

The Limits of Democracy

Soon after the Sandinistas' 1979 victory in Nicaragua, military and economic aid began to flood into Honduras. Long linked to the United States through the U.S.-owned banana enclaves, Honduras cemented a new relationship with Washington in the 1980s. In exchange for use of its territory for U.S. counterrevolutionary initiatives in the region, Honduras became a favored recipient of U.S. military and economic largesse. Almost overnight Honduras became one of the world's top ten recipients of U.S. foreign aid.

Along with its newly acquired geopolitical prominence, Honduras also experienced significant internal changes. The armed forces—which had since 1956 reserved for themselves a central role in governing the country—retired to their barracks, opening up the Casa Rosada (president's house in downtown Tegucigalpa) to civilian political leadership. Since 1982 three popularly elected civilian governments have administered the government. Yet even as the armed forces were handing over government to the country's two main political parties, Honduras was becoming visibly more militarized.

Never having been closely allied with an agroexport oligarchy, as has been the case elsewhere in the region, the Honduran military was not burdened with a history of brutal repression. The Honduran military, with intermittent civilian governments, had placed itself in position as the national institution that functioned as the country's final arbiter of power and the mediator of class conflicts. As such, it sponsored governments of national unity, an agrarian-reform process, and a national economic development plan that received the support of diverse social and economic sectors.

Like their counterparts in the region, the Honduran military and police have been imbued with a virulent anti-socialist ideology, but this counterinsurgency mentality never dominated military thinking and practice to the extent of its neighbors. Instead of worrying principally about defense against internal leftist subversion, Honduras has historically been more caught up in fear of invasion and in its own sense of inferiority vis-a-vis its neighbors, particularly El Salvador.

Although no longer in immediate control of the government structure, the military remains the most powerful national institution. During the 1980s the country's military and police forces gained a new sense of self-importance owing to increased U.S. aid and as a result of its embrace of the imperatives of the national-security doctrine.

Not only did the police and military become concerned about the infiltration of revolutionaries from surrounding states, but they became preoccupied over all signs of internal dissidence. In the 1980s, while Honduras moved successfully to what some political analysts have called a "formal democracy," it also became more like an armed camp and police state.[1] Police began checking citizen identification cards in city parks, military roadblocks became common, a sweeping anti-terrorist law was passed, rumors of basement torture chambers mounted, clandestine graves were found, and disappearances and killings of popular leaders became common. While the military and police were growing more repressive, they also were becoming more well equipped thanks to their U.S. benefactors and advisers.

The other sad irony of the 1980s was a boom of conspicuous consumption and luxury amid the steady decline of socioeconomic conditions.

Downtown in Tegucigalpa's Central Plaza unemployed men had replaced young boys in shining the shoes of the city's professionals and bureaucrats. But uptown dollars and *lempiras* now flowed along Morazán Boulevard — a new strip of luxury restaurants, U.S.-style fastfood outlets, and fancy shops. Hondurans talked about a "rain of dollars" pouring down on the government, military, and business elite from the U.S. embassy, the Pentagon, and the U.S. Agency for International Development (AID). New restaurants sprung up to cater to gringo corps of consultants, embassy personnel, evangelical missionaries, and intelligence agents.

While downtown and on the shack-covered hills of Tegucigalpa droves of young boys joined an epidemic of glue sniffing, the middle and upper classes increasingly tried to insulate themselves from the country's surging poverty and crime. Security services became the boom business of the 1980s. Although their homes are generally less imposing than the upper classes of El Salvador and Guatemala, the Honduran elite now also employ an army of private security guards brandishing shotguns and, increasingly, automatic weapons.

Per capita income — which currently stands at less than $800 a year — declined in the 1980s. Only one in ten Hondurans has what resembles a secure job. Even those holding jobs often cannot afford to meet their basic necessities since most unskilled laborers earn less than $2 a day. During the decade the purchasing power of Honduran workers dropped 30 percent. The cost of basic goods rapidly increased in late 1989 and early 1990 — so much so that *catrachas* (beans and shredded cabbage on a *tortilla*), the standard fare of many Hondurans, have become unaffordable.

During the 1980s Honduras became an increasingly polarized and violent society. As a result, the country's popular sectors have become more organized and militant. A popular movement of unions, peasant associations, and student groups which has formed an important part of Honduran society since the mid-1950s gained a new dimension in the 1980s with the appearance of human rights organizations, popular coalitions, and spontaneous community organizing. The demands of the popular movement have expanded from strictly economic and sectoral concerns to broader national issues such as militarization and foreign policy. Disappearances, arrests, and torture have not had the intended effect of silencing these dissidents. As in Guatemala and El Salvador, the cycle of repression and radicalization seems to widen and sharpen of its own almost inevitable momentum.

History of Dependence and Underdevelopment

Thrust into the geopolitical limelight during the 1980s, the historic flaws of the Honduran development process have acquired tragic new dimensions. The characteristics of the 1980s — dependency and subservience of the Honduran state, a paranoiac fear of its neighbors, militarization of politics, lack of a strong national identity, absence of a dynamic entrepreneurial spirit, unprincipled and narrowly based political parties, and pervasive corruption — were not products of the Reagan era but of deeply rooted problems that have long obstructed the political, social, and economic development of Honduras.

Long dominated by the U.S. banana giants — United Fruit and Standard Fruit — Honduras never developed a cohesive political and economic elite. Unlike most other Central American countries, the Liberal Party reforms of the 1870s did not spur the rise of a coffee oligarchy. It was not until the 1950s that the country began to significantly diversify its exports to include coffee, cotton, cattle, and sugar. The lack of a transportation infrastructure had been one obstacle to wider incorporation into the world economy. The territory's historic backwater status, lack of rich volcanic soils, isolation from world trade, and inability to form a strong national government are among other factors that obstructed Honduran economic advance.

Not having a large indigenous population and without an aristocratic coffee oligarchy, Honduras did not become as sharply stratified as neighboring countries. There long existed an economic elite, but it never reached the heights of wealth, exclusiveness, and political power seen elsewhere in Central America. In fact, it was not until the 1950s that powerful rancher and business organizations like the National Association of Growers and Cattlemen (FENAGH) and the Honduran Private Enterprise Council (COHEP) began to form.

Deep divisions, nonetheless, mark Honduran society, especially the traditional disjunction between rural and urban sectors. The peasantry has been relegated to the distant fringes of Honduran society — left uneducated and barely surviving on a diet of corn, beans, and sorghum. Among those who have found a decent life in the cities, there is a strong distaste for any manual work that smacks of the peasantry. At the same time, the Honduran *campesinos* have been less submissive than those in highly stratified and ethnically divided societies like Guatemala. Honduran *campesinos* have formed militant organizations to demand land and have joined in wider coalitions and confederations with trade unions.

No other Central American country is so flagrantly corrupt. The most readily observed and experienced example of this is the venality of the police. But pervasive corruption extends far beyond the public sector deep into the core of the business community, which often seems to survive by sopping up the revenues and resources of the government and foreign aid. Bolstered by Washington and its conservative free-market aid programs, the country's business elite has damned government inefficiency and corruption while proclaiming its own innate economic efficiency and integrity. Yet as former Minster of Labor Gautama Fonseca observed: "There is nothing more inefficient and corrupt in Honduras than private enterprise. They steal millions of dollars every year from the government, from the people. Now we're supposed to sell off our public enterprises at rock-bottom prices to the thieves and mafiosos who sucked the government dry to begin with."[2]

Separating business corruption from government corruption is an impossible task in Honduras where the private sector and political elite are often indistinguishable. This is particularly the case with the Callejas administration. Elected in November 1989, Rafael Leonardo Callejas is a wealthy businessman and banker who has also served as a director of many state enterprises. His cabinet is drawn largely from private-sector figures with strong ties to AID.

Also dipping generously into the public coffers and using public service to accumulate private fortunes are the military's officer corps. The influx into the country of over $1.6 billion in direct U.S. aid and hundreds of millions of dollars in contra assistance raised the scale of official corruption to new levels during the 1980s. Drug smuggling also became a lucrative new source of wealth during the decade. So permeated was Honduras by drug dollars that one Honduran judge called the country a "narco-state."[3]

During the 1980s Honduras played the perfect foreign-policy pawn — a role for which it was rewarded, although the U.S. dollars that the Honduran government and military received often fell short of what they demanded. Throughout the 1980s Honduras skillfully exploited its acquiescence to U.S. foreign-policy concerns to wrest continuing aid commitments from Washington while hedging on commitments to devaluate its currency, privatize its state enterprises, and institute harsher austerity measures. By so doing, the government managed to maintain a small measure of its historic commitment to the politics of social compromise.

Facing the Nineties

For the past ten years the country's acute internal problems were pushed into the background. The institutionalization of electoral politics and the anticommunist frenzy generated by the purported threat of a

Nicaraguan invasion served to downplay the seriousness of Honduran underdevelopment and poverty. Meanwhile, the vast influx of U.S. dollars in economic aid, contra support, and military assistance have kept the economy and government afloat while fortifying and enriching the armed forces and business elite.

Honduras, suffering from the regional turmoil of the 1980s, faces a yet more uncertain and troubled future in the 1990s. As long as the United States perceives popular movements as threatening to the established order in Central America, Washington will maintain its interventionist role in the region. The continued presence of the Sandinista opposition in Nicaragua and the persistence of leftist threats in El Salvador and Guatemala necessitate that Washington maintain Honduras as a close ally and platform for U.S. intervention. But U.S. budget constraints and changing foreign-policy priorities mean that Honduras will receive less in return for its cooperation. No longer can the government depend on a U.S. economic bailout, and the Honduran military will also find its budget cut back as U.S. military aid and contra money dwindle.

Domestic tensions are likely to rise as foreign aid drops and new austerity measures and business-oriented "reforms" take effect. Despite the election of three civilian presidents, the promise of democracy and civilian government faded in the 1980s as politicians oversaw the militarization of the country, the sale of national sovereignty, and the absence of social reforms. As elsewhere in Latin America, a popular challenge to the formal democracy in Honduras will likely characterize the country's future political arena. During the 1980s the country's unequal alliance with the United States had drawn it into the center of interventionist strategy for the region. In the 1990s, however, Honduras may find that the sharp social conflicts that have come to the forefront in surrounding countries will further complicate the task of governing in this desperately poor nation.

Chapter 1

Politics

Government

After 16 years of almost uninterrupted direct rule by the military, the 1980s saw the installation of elected civilians in the presidential palace. Today the casual observer in Honduras will see many signs of an apparently healthy democracy. Buildings and lamp posts are papered with posters from mainstream political campaigns and accented with graffiti by student groups of the left and right. Passionate debates expressing a broad spectrum of opinion flourish in the nation's daily press along with exposés and counterattacks by competing elite factions. Labor unions and *campesino* groups representing the poor majority press their demands and protest government policies in street demonstrations that typically meet little resistance from the authorities.

But piercing through this veneer of democracy are signs of a different nature. Heavily armed soldiers dressed in combat gear are posted on street corners throughout the major cities. Street children brazenly enter restaurants to beg for table scraps. Military intelligence and police units zoom down the busy streets of the capital in shiny late-model cars bearing no identification or license plates, their faces concealed behind dark, polarized windows.

Leaflets plastered along busy thoroughfares announce the formation of new "death squads" and list their intended victims among the country's civic leaders. Newspapers and broadcast media exercise their freedom amid constant acts of harassment and threats by the armed forces. Government officials are increasingly subject to public ridicule and outrage for so easily bending to the wishes of the armed forces and the U.S. embassy.

These contradictory images serve to underscore the incomplete nature of the democracy under construction in Honduras since 1980. For many Hondurans, such constraints and limitations are not measured against abstract democratic ideals, but rather against their historical experience prior to the 1980s. Seen in this light, the Liberal Party regimes of Roberto Suazo Córdova (1981-1985) and José Azcona Hoyo (1986-1990) have actually been less democratic in terms of the content of their policies and actions than some of the military regimes of the previous decades.

Between 1950 and 1980 the strategies of modernization and national development pursued by Honduran rulers often relied on notions of social compromise, limited reforms, and the politics of inclusion. Successive civilian and military governments over this period — acting sometimes under pressure from labor and *campesino* groups, sometimes in concert with them — adopted numerous reforms. These included progressive legislative reforms such as a labor code and agrarian-reform laws, as well as social-protection measures like price controls, subsidies on basic goods and services, and a welfare and social-security system. The reforms aimed at broadening the government's institutional base of support while seeking to avoid polarization or radicalization among the population in the face of deteriorating social and economic conditions.

Although sometimes ignored and other times trampled upon, the reforms nonetheless constituted important gains for the worker and peasant majorities and reflected the degree to which ruling elites attempted to govern by consent and compromise. Reformist sectors in the military were particularly keen on bringing the leaders of popular organizations into the policy-formation process, and at times displayed ample flexibility in terms of incorporating their demands.

Democratization and Militarization

The upsurge of revolutionary fervor in Central America at the end of the 1970s ushered in a new period of Honduran politics. In the months following the 1979 Sandinista victory in neighboring Nicaragua, the Carter administration worked out a plan with the Honduran military to return the government to civilian hands. Since 1980 a constituent assembly, a new constitution, the National Congress, and three civilian presidencies have been established through elections. Although there had also been mounting pressure inside Honduras for a change to civilian rule, and even the military itself was anxious to get out of the business of running the government, the shift was above all a product of U.S. designs.

Carter's project, later expanded by Reagan, was based on bolstering the Honduran armed forces so that they could guarantee the domestic peace and stability necessary to assume the role of regional staging ground for counterrevolution. A civilian administration and mild reforms were essential to gaining international legitimacy for the plan, and in the extreme it was hoped that Honduras could become a "showcase democracy."

Washington Post columnist Jack Anderson described Carter's strategy this way: "The president seems determined to add still another sorry chapter to the chronicle of Yankee imperialism in Central America. The administration apparently has chosen Honduras to be our new "Nicaragua" — a dependable satellite bought and paid for by American military and economic largesse. In secret meetings with the Pentagon's emissary...the Honduran military junta was told specifically that it is expected to assume the regional role played for years by Nicaragua's Anastasio Somoza — to become the bulwark of anticommunism against the pressure of popular revolt."[1]

While overseeing the post-1979 transition to civilian rule, General Policarpo Paz García ensured the military's continued dominance in Honduran politics. In October 1981 top leaders from the military and the country's two major political parties came to an agreement on the ground rules for the transition. The civilians committed themselves to noninterference in military affairs, including foreign-policy matters relating to national security and the country's borders and investigations into corruption under the previous military regimes. The military also retained veto power over cabinet appointments.[2]

Paz García's successor as military chief, General Gustavo Alvarez Martínez, erected a police state apparatus to control the domestic population and to help Washington mount a war against Nicaragua — all behind the curtain of elected civilian rule. Today the civilian president and Congress function largely in a public-relations role to explain and defend decisions made in the barracks, the banks, and the U.S. embassy.

Although the formal reins of government during the 1980s were in the hands of elected civilian leaders, both formal and informal arrangements assured a dominant role in the decision-making process for the military and the U.S. embassy. While these three protagonists have gone to great lengths to project an image of harmonious coexistence, the relationship has been fraught with jealous infighting and power plays. As one analyst put it: "Each actor has sought greater autonomy while attempting to reduce the jurisdiction and influence of the other two. This power struggle has formed the backdrop for Honduran politics since 1980."[3]

The image of Honduran rulers reluctantly giving in to U.S. pressures, or simply selling the country in exchange for massive amounts of aid is not entirely accurate. Throughout most of the 1980s the White House was able to work with Honduran leaders because their interests and agendas were largely consistent with U.S. policies. This was particularly the case within the armed forces high command—except for a brief interlude under General Walter López—which came to enjoy even greater power than under previous military governments. During his victory speech following the November 1989 elections, President Rafael Callejas hammered home the point that he can best serve Honduras as "a strong ally of the United States," since the two countries share similar objectives and thus "cooperation is mutually advantageous."[4]

Structure of Government[5]

Although the military and the United States are powerful behind-the-scenes actors, Honduras has succeeded in erecting a civilian state apparatus, backed up in theory by constitutional principles, responsible for carrying out policy decisions. The current Honduran Constitution—the fourteenth magna carta since independence in 1838—is the product of a National Constituent Assembly elected in 1980. While the Assembly worked on the document for over a year and a half, it introduced few substantial changes from the structure and pattern of government inherited from the previous decades. Formal power is concentrated in a highly centralized state apparatus headed by a strong executive branch. Although in spirit the constitution subscribes to the principle of separation of powers, the executive dominates both the legislative and judicial branches. Likewise, the potential for autonomy at the local level has been blocked by centralization of authority.

In part, the executive's influence derives from the power of appointment: the president is responsible for naming all major cabinet officers (subject to approval of the military) as well as the 18 departmental governors who oversee the activities of local government bodies. Technically, the Congress is responsible for appointing the chief of the armed forces, as well as members of the Supreme Court, but in practice it has always rubber-stamped the military's proposed candidate.

The executive branch also presides over the burgeoning state apparatus and the assignment of posts in the public sector which constitutes the core of political patronage for the parties. By 1984 there were an estimated 70,000 employees working for the national government. These include traditional ministries and departments, such as education, the military, the central bank, and utilities, as well as a wide array of decentralized agencies covering affairs like agrarian reform, housing, and forestry development. Traditionally, following each change government, the victors awarded thousands of their supporters with state jobs. As a sign of the changing times, soon after assuming office in early 1990, the Callejas administration sent dismissal notices to some 6,000 public employees. But this time the vacancies were not filled by National Party militants and campaign workers; the new president's austerity package plans an across-the-board reduction of 10 percent in the public workforce.

In 1989 a total of 128 representatives were elected to the unicameral National Congress where they serve four-year terms. Historically in Honduras — and the "new democracy" of the 1980s was no exception — the Congress rarely challenges executive authority. "The great problems that afflict Honduran society," lamented Christian Democratic Congressman Efraín Díaz Arrivillaga, "namely the problems of human rights, foreign policy and the economy, are rarely debated in the Congress. The Congress legitimizes all the executive wants. Practically speaking, it is not an independent power; it does not maintain any control over the executive."[6]

The judicial system is administered by a nine-member congressionally appointed Supreme Court. The Supreme Court is empowered to intervene in cases involving questions of constitutionality. In practice, the court's effectiveness and independence have been circumscribed by party loyalty, executive influence, widespread corruption, and the continuing impunity of the military. A graphic example of the court's limited authority occurred on July 4, 1987, when a Supreme Court magistrate was shot and killed by a police trooper after reportedly failing to stop at a roadblock. Although the Supreme Court called for the trooper's arrest and trial in the civilian courts, the military prevailed with its insistence on dealing with the affair internally.[7]

The government structure is rounded out by 289 municipal representatives and the highly politicized National Election Board, responsible for overseeing all electoral matters. Voting is mandatory for all citizens, with the exception of active military personnel who are not allowed to vote. Only the president is elected by direct vote. Congressional and municipal seats are assigned on the basis of party slates and vote proportions. Labor unions and other popular organizations have called for democratic reforms in the electoral legislation to allow voters to directly chose candidates for Congress and local posts, as opposed to the current, more restrictive system of party slates.

Political Parties and Elections

Party politics in Honduras have historically been dominated by *caudillos* (strongmen), with ideology taking a back seat to questions of personalism and influence.[8] Although newer generations of Honduran politicians have attempted to modify this tradition somewhat, the essence remains the same. This was especially apparent during the 1989 presidential campaign which relied far more on imagery and machine politics than ideology or a programmatic platform.

The two dominant political forces—the Liberal Party (PL) and the National Party (PN)—emerged around the turn of this century. Both had close ties to the U.S. fruit companies which dominated national life and politics: the PN was close to the United Fruit Company, while the Liberals were partisan to the Cuyamel Fruit Company.

Through a complex series of legal obstacles, as well as through traditional loyalties among the population, the Liberals and Nationals have all but made it impossible for newer parties to challenge their predominance. With the revolutionary left outlawed and moderate or progressive forces small and marginalized, party politics remain dominated by the two big parties, whose stances on the major issues of the day are not substantially different. As a result, since the 1950s popular organizations and trade unions have played an essential role in pressing the demands and grievances of the worker and peasant majorities.

Red and White or White and Blue?

"Vote for me, I'll be watching you on elections day," proclaimed Rafael Callejas to a group of illiterate peasants in Comayagua during his 1989 presidential campaign. "I'll be the last one on the ballot, the one with glasses and no mustache, that's Callejas."[9] With the tradition of bipartisan politics firmly established, and few substantive issues around which to distinguish themselves, the contending presidential candidates in 1989 had to expend much of their campaign energies attempting to differentiate themselves in the eyes of the electorate. Proposals to have the candidates' photographs removed from the ballot were quickly beaten back.

As another part of his effort to capture the *campesino* vote, Callejas secured the use of a helicopter which he used to shuttle from one remote mountain village to another to make brief appearances. In the cities, one of Callejas' main tactics was to rail against the bureaucracy and inefficiency of the previous Liberal regimes, promising to reduce the size and role of the government, particularly in the economy.

In many ways, Callejas' victory at the polls by an impressive margin was due to his efforts to modernize the National Party and revamp its appeal to voters. But for the most part Honduran political parties work as they did 40 or 50 years ago. From the longstanding identification of the electorate with party colors—the National's are blue and white, the

Liberal's red and white — to the handing down from generation to generation of party preferences among the electorate, political traditions die hard. Similarly, party strength remains highly dependent upon the ability to dole out jobs in the public sector. On election days, a given candidate's ability to provide food and transportation to polling places for potential sympathetic voters can still be decisive.[10]

The founding members of the National Party (PN), who split from the Liberals in 1902, were closely tied to large landed interests and historically the party has allied itself with the armed forces. Today the party represents conservative sectors of the business class and the state bureaucracy, and it continues to wield voting power among conservative sectors of the peasantry. Its current leader, the articulate Rafael Leonardo Callejas, won the November 1989 elections with over 50 percent of the vote. The 48-year-old Callejas is one of the youngest presidents in Honduran history.

Callejas, an agricultural economist, banker, and investor who was schooled in the United States, has expanded the traditional political machine — essentially peons voting for the landlord's party — to include a neoconservative movement. This movement is the Honduran version of a New Right, involving many young, first-time voters.

Although the PN led by Callejas does not yet have a strong ideological definition, it is decidedly to the right of center on the Honduran political spectrum and enjoys close ties with the ruling ARENA party in El Salvador and other rightwing forces in Central America.[11] Since the early 1980s the competing factions within the National Party — particularly that of former university rector Oswaldo Ramos Soto (Callejas' choice to head the Supreme Court) — have not mounted a serious challenge to Callejas' control of the party apparatus.

Traditionally, the Liberals had a broader support base than their National Party rivals, including a sector of conservative landowners, small farmers and the rural middle class, the more progressive urban-based professionals, and some bankers and business people. The Liberal Party historically has advocated curbs on the military's role in national life and greater government intervention in the economy, especially through limited land reform, job creation through public investment, and expansion of social services.

During this decade, both presidents and the majority in Congress have been from the Liberal Party. But the Liberal governments of the 1980s broke with the party's historic image, presiding over a massive military buildup, curbing reform initiatives, and at least partially carrying out harsh austerity measures demanded by the U.S. Agency for International Development (AID) and the International Monetary Fund (IMF). Progressive forces within the party have been increasingly marginalized.

The Liberal Party remains highly factionalized. One of Honduras' most famous *caudillos*, Modesto Rodas Alvarado, died in 1979. Dr. Roberto Suazo Córdova took his place as leader of the party's conservative mainstream *rodista* faction and went on to win the presidency in 1981. Four years later, José Azcona won over many disaffected *rodistas* and allied himself with the progressive, modernizing faction based among the North Coast industrialists who belong to the Liberal Alliance of the People (ALIPO) faction. There is another weak faction to the left of ALIPO, the Liberal Democratic Revolutionary Movement (M-LIDER), which espouses social-democratic positions and has been an outspoken force against the contra and U.S. military occupations. Representatives from all three factions vied for the 1989 Liberal Party nomination, with the *rodistas'* Carlos Flores Facussé eventually winning.

Two minority parties have enjoyed small representation in Congress in the 1980s but have yet to build a national challenge to Liberal-National dominance. In 1989 together they won less than 3.5 percent of the vote. One is the center-left Innovation and Unity Party (PINU), which in 1988 affiliated itself with the Social Democratic International. The PINU was first formed in 1970, but did not acquire legal status until 1978. As a result of the 1989 elections, the PINU has two deputies in the National Congress.

The other minority party is the Christian Democratic Party of Honduras (PDCH). Similar in name only to the parties in El Salvador, Guatemala, and elsewhere in Latin America, Honduran Christian Democracy grew out of *campesino* movements and post-Vatican II "Popular Church" social and educational projects of the late 1960s through the mid-1970s. (See Religion) For years, the PDCH was linked to the powerful General Confederation of Workers (CGT) union federation, which is now dominated by its ties to the National Party, and to the affiliated National Peasant Union (UNC), which is currently divided into two factions. The party began its search for legal status in 1975, but it was not granted until after the 1980 constituent assembly elections. Despite the challenge of conservative elements within its ranks, the PDCH has managed to stay close to its progressive roots. Together with the more centrist PINU, the PDCH often acts as the "conscience" of the Honduran Congress by exposing corrupt, illegal, and unpatriotic actions of the powers that be. Receiving fewer votes in 1989 than in the previous elections, the PDCH lost its two representatives in Congress.

The progressive Frente Patriótico Hondureño (FPH) coalition ran candidates in the 1981 and 1982 elections, but failed to win a seat. After a long period of relative inactivity, interest in the coalition is again on the rise and the FPH is currently seeking legal recognition as a party to enter the 1994 elections.

The Communist Party of Honduras (PCH), which traces its roots back to the 1920s, was declared illegal in 1957, and it has never been allowed to participate directly in elections. In 1967 dissidents broke off to form a Marxist-Leninist faction, the PCH-ML. Both the PCH and the FPH are said to have ties to trade unions, peasant groups, and guerrilla organizations.

Elections in the Eighties

As the 1970s drew to a close, a centerpiece of the U.S. plan to convert Honduras into a stable bulwark against the advances of revolutionary forces in the isthmus was the installation of a civilian government through elections. Although three rounds of general elections were indeed held in the 1980s, the emergence of real democracy in Honduras has been stifled by the militarization of the nation's affairs, and by the extent to which the U.S. embassy and the armed forces continue to influence key decisions.[12]

Indeed Honduras is a prime example of the limitations in using the formal holding of elections as a yardstick of democracy. Under the elected civilian governments of the 1980s, Hondurans witnessed a reduction of traditional political spaces, a dramatic increase in repression and human rights abuses, and the closing of many avenues for peaceful change and reform. The policies adopted during this period—particularly in the key areas of the economy, defense, and foreign relations—were often at odds with popular sentiments on the issues. Many Hondurans remember the track record of earlier governments—both military and civilian, constituted and elected—whose sponsorship of reform initiatives provided them with greater legitimacy as "democratic" regimes than the modern-day "cleanly elected" leaders.[13]

Throughout this period the Honduran population's confidence in elections as a vehicle for authentic democratization and empowerment has eroded. In 1981 Hondurans enthusiastically participated in the first direct elections for president in over 25 years. The winner, Liberal Party candidate Roberto Suazo Córdova, a country doctor and rancher, was given an overwhelming mandate based on ambitious campaign promises to meet a series of popular demands. "This is a vote against corruption and the presence of the military in power," editorialized the liberal daily

Tiempo. "It is a vote in favor of a change in political style and of neutrality in the regional war."[14]

Four years later, a series of factors had led to widespread disenchantment with the government. Among them were: Suazo's cozy relations with the military and the United States, his abandonment of proclaimed Honduran "neutrality" regarding conflicts in the region, rampant corruption, attempts to unconstitutionally prolong his stay in office, and the deteriorating economic situation. All of this contributed to the electoral victory of Liberal Party rival José Azcona under the assumption that he would break with the unpopular policies of his predecessor and return to the traditional stances of the party. Azcona also made explicit campaign promises to rid Honduras of the contra presence during his term in office. Four years later the contras were still camped in Honduras, human rights violations were again on the rise, and popular discontent over the government's economic policies had sharpened.

In 1989 the electorate once again expressed its disappointment over the previous administration, this time by voting National Party candidate Callejas into office. Although voting is technically mandatory, abstention was calculated at over 23 percent of the electorate, up 6 percent from the 1985 elections in a clear expression of growing apathy.[15] Apparently many Hondurans had become skeptical about the electoral process and the nature of the democracy it represented.

Widespread irregularities in the electoral process itself, particularly regarding the selection of candidates within the parties and problems in voter registration, led to both major parties exchanging incessant charges of fraud. Furthermore, backroom deals between the two parties and with the military severely constrained the power of elected officials.

The 1981 elections, for example, were preceded by a pact which would assure certain levels of power and influence for the military after the transition to civilian rule. Even with this agreement in hand, the campaign period was marred by rumors of a military coup backed by extreme right politicians and sectors of the National Party, and by calls for postponement of the elections by the centrist parties due to irregularities in the voter registration lists.[16]

Similarly, the 1985 elections took place on the heels of a constitutional crisis produced when President Suazo Córdova attempted first to engineer a second term in office for himself, and when that failed, to impose a hand-picked successor as the Liberal Party candidate. Anti-Suazo forces in Congress fired the pro-Suazo Supreme Court, which in turn charged the Congress with treason. Suazo retaliated by ordering the arrest of the newly appointed judges and dispatching the elite counterinsurgency Cobra forces to surround the Congress and Supreme Court buildings. Only the massive pressure brought to bear by an unprecedented ad-hoc alliance — stretching from factions of the National Party to progressive politicians and trade unions — backed by the threat of a general strike, coupled with the mediating efforts of armed forces chief General Walter López and threats by the United States to cut off aid to Honduras if the "democratic image" became tarnished, convinced Suazo to back down.[17]

Suazo's Liberal Party rival Azcona became president in 1985 in part as a result of a deal which was struck in the wake of the constitutional crisis. To overcome the party infighting over candidate nomination which had led to the crisis, it was agreed that any and all party factions could run candidates in the elections and the one from the party with the highest combined total of votes would become president. Nine candidates eventually appeared on the ballot in November, and the National Party's Callejas took the lion's share with 41 percent of the votes. Because the total number of Liberal Party votes for president was 49 percent, Azcona, who personally had only won 27 percent, was declared president.

Displeased with this outcome but reluctant to call for new elections, the National Party forced Azcona to share power by placing the Judicial Branch, the Ministry of Foreign Relations, and other key cabinet posts under National Party control. While the new government was obviously a hybrid, the details of the Pact of National Unity were kept from the public for over a year and as the government became increasingly unpopular, the National Party began denying its share of responsibility in hopes of clearing its name before the 1989 elections. Nonetheless, the pact underscored the fact that few political differences of importance separate the majority factions of the two parties.[18]

Once again, the 1989 elections were fraught with irregularities, uncertainties and mutual charges of fraud.[19] This time, controversy centered on widespread irregularities in voter registration lists, including reports of tens of thousands of deceased persons and several thousand foreigners listed on the voter rolls. The U.S. Agency for International Development (AID) earmarked $4 million of its $10 million election package for voter registration activities and a purge of the electoral register, but even this failed to eradicate the abnormalities.

In the days before the vote President Azcona charged that U.S. officials were meddling in the electoral process. Shortly after the elections presidential spokesman Marco Tulio Romero announced Azcona's decision to not accept the credentials of the new U.S. ambassador to Honduras, Crecensio Arcos, charging that CIA and AID agents, under the guise of "electoral advisers," had tampered with voter registration lists to ensure a Callejas victory.[20] The Liberal Party also accused AID of helping to assure an opposition victory by witholding a $70 million disbursement in previously approved aid, a move which led to visible economic difficulties for the Azcona government during the campaign period.

Although he counts on a large public mandate with a 51 to 43 percent victory over the Liberals and on a large majority in Congress, Callejas assumed office in January 1990 under difficult circumstances.[21] Callejas will come under intense pressure from AID and the IMF to devalue the national currency and implement further austerity measures, moves which can be expected to provoke a response from the popular opposition which grew in the latter half of the 1980s. Likewise, the hoped-for control over the military does not seem to be in the cards. Although the National Party has largely succeeded in burying its longstanding image as the "civilian wing of the armed forces," Callejas himself was a founding member of APROH, the far-right organization set up by General Alvarez in 1983 to act as a civilian-military pressure group. He also served as a high-level official in the military governments of the 1970s.

The first major disappointment with the new government came with Callejas' announcement of cabinet appointments in early 1990. Since his November 1989 victory, Callejas had been publicly stressing his intentions to form a "government of national reconciliation," based on a consensus among the country's principal political and social forces. Although the new president gave representatives of the defeated Liberal Party three seats in the leadership of the National Congress, as well as three of the nine Supreme Court magistrates, all key ministries are in the hands of close Callejas associates. Significantly, the top three economic positions—ministers of the economy and the treasury and president of the Central Bank—all went to technocrats from Callejas' inner circle who have worked closely with AID.

Foreign Policy

The fundamental dynamic in Honduran foreign policy over the past 15 years has been the tendency of the civilian and military leadership to define national interests as a function of U.S. strategy for Central America.[22] As a result, traditional adversaries were transformed into "allies" (El Salvador); new "enemies" emerged (Nicaragua); and a country described in 1982 as an "oasis of peace" (Honduras) was turned into a perpetual base for two foreign armies (the U.S. and the contras) and a temporary training site for a third (Salvadoran). This "denationalization" of foreign policy led to a growing outcry among the public and important institutions of Honduran society while isolating the country internationally. By the end of the 1980s combined pressures forced the government to reconsider the key issue of contra presence in Honduran territory.

Honduras' relations within Central America have always been influenced by the country's central geographic position on the isthmus. For centuries Honduran territory—which shares long borders with Guatemala, El Salvador, and Nicaragua—has alternately played the role of battleground, staging area, and rearguard for regional conflicts.

It was in large part due to this strategic location that at the beginning of this century the theoretical cornerstone of Honduran foreign policy was defined as perpetual neutrality vis-a-vis conflicts in the rest of Central America. Formally, the principle of neutrality has never been abandoned. But in practice it has been progressively distorted and stripped of its contents by the string of military governments which have ruled during most of this century, and more recently by increasing alignment with the United States. By the mid-1980s Honduran foreign-policy concerns had largely been reduced to mere reflections of U.S. regional strategy.

The intermingling of U.S. and Honduran foreign-policy interests goes back to the banana empire days when the fruit companies' control over local politics ensured that the nation's foreign policy would not stray too far from Washington's desires. Although more nationalist-minded sectors have since emerged and the relationship with the United States has become much more complex, the pattern has not been broken. Honduran collaboration with the United States in the 1954 overthrow of the Arbenz government in Guatemala and in anti-Castro adventures in the 1960s find their counterparts in more recent years in the contra war and support for the Salvadoran military's campaign against the FMLN guerrillas.

Peace Zone or Garrison State?

In his inaugural speech in January 1982, newly elected President Roberto Suazo Córdova outlined the principal tenets of the civilian government's proposed foreign policy: "Central America ought to be an area of peaceful coexistence in which its peoples and leaders may establish and maintain an understanding through dialogue, and a peace zone free of the torment of war and polarizing confrontations....Honduras does not intend to become a referee of regional expectations, anguish, and hopes. But it does yearn, faithful to the principles of non-intervention and self-determination, to become a factor for stability and concord."[23] In the ensuing months, as General Alvarez consolidated the military's authority over the civilian government and began implementing U.S. designs for the country, the gap between the principles enunciated by Suazo Córdova and the reality of Honduran foreign policy widened into a gulf.

At first, this dynamic took the form of a two-headed foreign policy in Honduras. As then-chief of staff of the armed forces Colonel Efraín González noted: "Military operations were carried out with foreign troops without asking the permission of the Congress or the president. At times the foreign policy of the country went in one direction and the armed forces in another."[24] Although for a short period some in the civilian administration attempted to resist the tendency of subordination to the military's dictates, the deck was clearly stacked against them. After the ouster of Alvarez in 1984, the foreign minister himself conceded: "I know that in the past there have been certain irregularities that didn't depend on the president nor the minister of foreign relations, because General Alvarez had his own opinions and also carried on his own foreign policy with a kind of cabinet hidden in a shady cloak of association called APROH. That is the reality."[25]

The Suazo period accelerated a trend already underway whereby the formulation of Honduran foreign policy had been gradually shifting from the political party in power to the military and to private pressure groups. One of the conditions the military imposed as part of the 1980-1981 transition to civilian government was that the armed forces would be allowed to maintain authority over the definition of key aspects of foreign policy. The military-dominated National Security Council is responsible for defining the broad contours of the nation's foreign policy. (See Security Forces) The military high command often makes strategic decisions relating to foreign affairs and later presents these decisions to the president and National Congress as *fait accompli*.[26]

The most influential pressure group which had a role in defining foreign policy during this period was the Association for the Progress of Honduras (APROH). Formed in January 1983 with General Alvarez at the helm, APROH was an alliance of far-right military, business and political elites and conservative labor and peasant groups. Described by congressional opposition leader Efraín Díaz as "the center of power in Honduras," APROH operated as a think tank which turned out elaborate policy proposals, particularly regarding the economy and foreign relations.

When the Kissinger Commission visited the isthmus in 1983, for example, it was APROH, not the ruling Liberal Party, that wrote the official documents for presentation to the Commission. Already suffering from widespread popular rejection for its links to CAUSA, the political wing of the Moonies, APROH fell apart in the wake of the ouster of Alvarez in 1984.[27] Although Alvarez and APROH have long since departed, their imprint on Honduran politics remains strong. In fact, several top cabinet posts in the National Party government which came out of the 1989 elections went to key figures from APROH, an organization in which President Callejas himself played a leading role.

General Walter López and the other military officers who replaced Alvarez attempted to put a more nationalistic face on relations with the United States and foreign-policy issues in general. But in the end their efforts were largely reduced to extracting a greater price in U.S. aid in exchange for the role the country was playing. "Most of this is smoke," said one U.S. diplomat referring to Honduran demands for a $3 billion aid package. "The new bunch is trying to show they are in charge....But we haven't been turned down on anything we've asked from them."[28] Indeed, although most of the Honduran demands were at best met halfway by Washington, foreign policy continued its course much as before.

As the Central American crisis deepened over the 1980s, Honduran foreign policy shifted through several overlapping phases. Early in the decade the country was converted into the principal staging ground for the Reagan administration's regional counterrevolution. The installation of contra bases on Honduran territory and collaboration between the Honduran and Salvadoran armed forces in the war against the FMLN were the most salient manifestations of this new regional role. Beginning with the Contadora peace negotiations in 1983 and later with the Esquipulas II Peace Accords of 1987, the country's cooperation with U.S. interventionism became increasingly embarrassing and untenable. Honduras' persistent stalling tactics during the process of regional negotiations led to a deterioration of the country's image in Central America and internationally.

By 1988 a combination of pressures forced the government to shift its position vis-a-vis the contra presence and to provide at least lukewarm support for efforts to demobilize the contra army. Honduras' constant vacillations about the demobilization indicate, however, that this change in policy is due more to political expediency and realpolitick than to any fundamental questioning of its overall relationship with the United States. On the one hand, by the end of the 1980s even sectors of the Honduran elite recognized the destabilizing effect of the contra presence. On the other, both the military and the politicians became convinced that U.S. aid levels would not diminish significantly as a result of a hard-line stance in favor of contra demobilization.

The overall tendency to define foreign policy in line with U.S. concerns has not resulted in the elimination of old issues, nor has it precluded the emergence of new international actors. Many Honduran foreign-policy issues that do not fit neatly with U.S. interests hail back to the disastrous 1969 war with El Salvador. The brief armed conflict, sometimes known as the "Soccer War," erupted as a result of long-standing border tensions owing to an ill-defined demarcation, the Honduran expulsion of some 100,000 Salvadoran immigrants, and domestic political and economic pressures in both countries. The Salvadoran army invaded Honduras and advanced rapidly, while the Honduran air force retaliated with successful strikes on key Salvadoran installations. Four days later, the OAS arranged a cease-fire and international observers were sent to the zone.

Despite formal establishment of a three kilometer-wide demilitarized zone in 1970, negotiations remained stalled at the cease-fire level. Sporadic fighting between the two countries and an unresolved state of war persisted until 1980 when the Carter administration pushed through the signing of a provisional peace treaty between the two countries. Nonetheless, the actual border dispute which gave rise to the conflict in the first place remains unresolved.[29] Bad blood between the two countries persists to this day despite Washington's efforts to focus Honduran attention on "Soviet-Cuban threats" from the Sandinistas and the FMLN to diffuse the traditional enmity. Honduras negotiated the 1987 purchase of advanced U.S. fighter jets partly to ensure air superiority over El Salvador.

Peace Process

Prior to the August 1987 Esquipulas II Peace Accords, Honduras, along with El Salvador, acted repeatedly in concert with the United States to scuttle peace initiatives in the region. Recent exceptions to this pattern respond to intense internal and international pressures to demobilize the Honduras-based contra army. As for other aspects of the peace process, such as national dialogue and respect for human rights, Honduras has made little if any progress as the country's leaders insist that such clauses "do not apply to Honduras."

Under President Suazo Córdova, Honduran foreign minister Edgardo Paz Barnica took the lead among Central Americans boycotting regional peace efforts at the behest of Washington both before and after the preliminary Contadora accords of 1984. But three years later, with the emergence of the Esquipulas peace process, radically changed conditions in the region and in Washington led to the partial abandonment of Honduras' role as spoiler of regional peace initiatives, particularly regarding the crucial issue of demobilization of the contras.[30] The February 1990 electoral victory by the UNO coalition in Nicaragua removed many of the obstacles which had contributed to Honduran foot-dragging on contra demobilization, but the Callejas administration seemed more interested in letting Washington, UNO, and the Sandinistas deal with removing the contras from Honduran territory.

Contras Overstay their Welcome

In the early 1980s many Honduran leaders supported contra use of Honduran territory under the assumption that it would be a short-term affair and that the occasional presence of a few bands of ex-Somoza guardsmen along the border with Nicaragua would go largely unnoticed. But by 1986 some 40,000 contras and their families, unable to establish a presence inside Nicaragua, had literally taken over a 450 square kilometer area in southern Honduras. Contra patrols at the entrance points to what they called "New Nicaragua" decided who was allowed to enter and who was not.[31] (See Refugees and the Internally Displaced)

In 1986-1987 severe military defeats suffered by contra forces inside Nicaragua erased any remaining hopes for a contra military victory and brought thousands of contra fighters back to their bases in southern Honduras. Popular pressures inside Honduras to expel the contras were reaching unmanageable levels. Anti-contra sentiments began to reach into sectors of the military, the traditional political parties, and the business elite — some of whom felt that Honduras had received far too little in U.S. aid in return. By the time of the Esquipulas II Peace Accords in late 1987, the Iran-Contra scandal in Washington and the drawing to a close of the Reagan years made Honduran leaders increasingly fearful that they would be left to pick up the pieces of the contra debacle.

The Honduran military, which had played a key role in supporting and safeguarding the contras' presence in the country in part on the assumption that it was a way to assure greater levels of U.S. military aid for the Honduran armed forces, had become increasingly alienated with the contra presence. Nationalistic sectors resented the existence of a "rival" army on national territory and feared the destabilizing consequences of thousands of contras roving around Honduras after a potential cutoff in U.S. aid. To make matters worse, when AID took over distribution of the contra aid program in 1988, it ceased to be a lucrative source of income for the Honduran officers who had been serving as intermediaries. A State Department official admitted in mid-1988 that the Honduran armed forces "will back a *modus vivendi* with the Sandinista government, independent of U.S. concerns."[32]

Following Azcona's August 1987 signing of the Esquipulas II Peace Accords, Honduras' role in the development and refinement of demobilization plans became inconsistent. Honduran vacillation on this point reflected both the lack of consensus in the government and military over how and when demobilization should take place, and the extent to which pressures by Washington continued to take their toll. "As long as the Americans are willing to foot the bill for the contras and continue to help us with military and economic aid," said one Honduran official in early 1989, "I don't think there will be a major problem in housing the contras."[33]

In late 1987 foreign minister Carlos López Contreras addressed the OAS and proposed a plan for demobilizing the contras. Taken outside the framework of the Esquipulas accords, the move was seen largely as a diplomatic ploy to symbolically announce Honduran intentions to comply with an eventual demobilization plan.

It was not until the February 1989 Costa del Sol summit, after a year and a half of backpedaling and stalling, that Azcona accepted demobilization to be determined by the five presidents. One surprised observer commented that perhaps for the first time, Azcona was acting "like the president of a sovereign country."[34] The turnaround was largely due to Washington's refusal to accept Honduran demands that the United States assume ultimate responsibility for the disarming and relocation of the contras.

Three months later, the Central American foreign vice-ministers, meeting in Guatemala City, came up with a draft demobilization plan which called for the creation of an International Verification Commission which would include the Secretary Generals of the UN and the OAS. After another round of Honduran stalling, in an August 1989 meeting in Tela Honduras, the five presidents agreed on a concrete demobilization plan to be carried out by December 5 under the auspices of a UN peacekeeping force. In January 1990 Azcona—who had been elected four years earlier largely on the basis of a campaign promise to rid Honduras of the contras—turned over the presidential sash to Rafael Callejas, while the defiant contras remained in their camps in the south.

Following through on its demobilization commitment has been difficult for Honduras for two reasons. First, the Bush administration, in open opposition to the deadlines specified in the peace accords signed by the five Central American presidents, pressured Honduras into accepting the presence of the bulk of contra forces until after the February 25, 1990 elections in Nicaragua. The original Esquipulas II Peace Accords, as well as subsequent agreements on postponing the deadline, all called for the contras to demobilize and return to Nicaragua *before* the elections, a stance which Washington never accepted. Second, the peace plan calls for "voluntary" demobilization, yet most contras simply refused to leave, even in the wake of the UNO electoral victory when Washington, the Sandinistas, UNO, and Honduras joined in a chorus urging them to do so. By the end of March 1990, with all of their support lines cut off, eventual repatriation for the majority of contras seemed inevitable. Most of the remaining contras began to trickle back into Nicaragua.

National Reconciliation and Dialogue

In the immediate aftermath of Esquipulas, there was widespread optimism in Honduras that, in addition to expulsion of the contras, the peace process would contribute to greater political openings, a drop in human rights abuses, and some form of national reconciliation to offset the growing polarization. Just weeks after the August 1987 signing of the accords, the Honduran Bishops' Conference issued a declaration in support of the treaty, calling on the Azcona government to move swiftly in the formation of a National Reconciliation Commission (CNR). The document affirmed that, among other issues, the CNR should promote a deepening of the democratic process through greater popular participation, ensure an end to human rights abuses, examine the refugee situation, and deal with the unwanted presence of the contras.[35] In addition to the church, business groups, political parties, trade unions, popular organizations, and even the guerrillas made public their suggestions for a host of problems which they felt should be addressed by the CNR.

But it was not until two days before the November 5 deadline stipulated in the treaties that the government officially formed the CNR. Over the next two years, the CNR held several meetings and there was even talk of holding a broad national dialogue aimed at creating a consensus around pressing economic and political problems, but substantive accords were never reached.

Although the government's lack of enthusiasm inhibited the CNR from playing a more aggressive role, the process did provide a public platform for the expression of discontent over the direction of national policy in key areas such as the economy, human rights, agrarian reform, and the U.S. military presence. In August 1988, for example, the CNR presented Azcona with a list of demands including a call to abolish the police investigations unit National Investigations Division (DNI), to overhaul the judicial system, and to redesign the agrarian-reform program.[36] Even the military presented a controversial communique to the CNR declaring that the economic model followed by the previous two administrations had come to a dead end and calling for a new strategy more reliant on agriculture and with greater employment-generating opportunities.[37]

Human Rights

Honduras has the distinction of being the only Latin American state ever convicted in a court of law for the crime of disappearance. Faced with this and other accusations of systematic human rights abuses during the 1980s—including torture, disappearances, extrajudicial executions, and widespread restrictions on civil liberties—Honduran civilian and military authorities have contended that the situation in their country pales in comparison to the climate of terror which reigns in neighboring El Salvador and Guatemala. Honduran defenders of human rights counter that the focus on *numbers* of violations misses the point. Beyond the fact that the only acceptable number is zero, the real issue is that a pattern of violations has continued unabated throughout the decade, and that it constitutes a systematic and deliberate policy carried out by the military and sanctioned by the civilian government.

The state's role in violations of human rights is nowhere more clearly proven than in the case of Honduras. Overwhelming evidence indicates that it is the military—not rightwing vigilantes—who carry out the violations. The initial wave of abuses took place from 1982-1984 when the armed forces were led by General Gustavo Alvarez. As early as 1982, an Americas Watch mission to Honduras reported that "the practice of arresting individuals for political reasons, and then refusing to acknowledge their whereabouts and status, seems to have become established in Honduras."[38] The report added that many of the disappeared had been taken to clandestine prisons and tortured.

It was under the aegis of the policies implemented by Alvarez in the framework of national-security doctrine (See Security Forces) that the isolated occurrences which had characterized the 1960s and 1970s—the murder and torture of trade-union and peasant organizers, arbitrary detentions, and several massacres—were replaced by a systematic policy, practiced selectively and clandestinely, of domestic repression. By the time of his ouster in March 1984, Alvarez had presided over 214 political assassinations, 110 disappearances, and 1,947 illegal detentions.[39] To a large extent, the "dirty war" succeeded in its goal of intimidation. "Hondurans gradually submitted to collective fear and paralysis," described one analyst. "The impunity with which the state's repressive forces acted made the population feel defenseless; many chose the complicity of silence, daring to share fears and opinions only with close friends."[40]

Widespread hopes that the departure of Alvarez would lead to an improvement in the situation and the prosecution of at least some of those involved in the earlier abuses were short-lived. The "dirty war" is over and Hondurans have been allowed a greater degree of political expression. But after a brief period of relative decline in human rights violations, and in spite of intense international scrutiny and legal action, since 1986 a resurgence in both the frequency and intensity of abuses has approached the extreme levels experienced in the first years of the decade. Independent human rights monitoring organizations report that disappearances have largely been supplanted by political assassinations.

Honduras Tried and Convicted

The violations of the early 1980s were aired in the Inter-American Court on Human Rights (IACHR) after years of official denials, refusals to investigate, and simple obstructions of justice.[41] This judicial arm of the OAS is composed of seven prominent jurists — six Latin and one North American — as judges. The court heard three cases against Honduras in its precedent-setting trial of a member state and the first juridical treatment of the crime of political disappearance.

The cases were brought to trial on behalf of the the families of disappearance victims by the OAS' human rights monitoring and legal action team, the Inter-American Commission on Human Rights. While the Commission prosecuted only three cases involving four individuals (two Hondurans and two Costa Ricans) "disappeared" by Honduran security forces during the 1981-1984 period, to do so it had to prove that the Honduran state "conducted or tolerated the systematic practice of disappearance" during that period.

The Commission called witnesses including independent Honduran human rights monitors, relatives of the victims, "disappearance" survivors, and a former member of Battalion 3/16 — a unit of the Honduran military created with CIA assistance and singled out by much of the evidence brought before the court as the chief group responsible for political executions and disappearances.[42]

After tense and lengthy proceedings the IACHR found the Honduran state guilty in the two cases involving Hondurans (verdicts of July 29, 1988 in the Manfredo Velásquez case and January 20, 1989 in the Saul Godínez case), but was forced to dismiss the case involving two Costa Ricans for lack of evidence. The IACHR ordered the government to pay "fair damages" to the victims' families. Its ruling concluded that the crimes against the two Hondurans constituted part of "a practice of disappearances carried out or tolerated by Honduran officials...between 1981 and

1984." The victims of that practice, according to the Court, numbered between 100 and 150."[43]

The Azcona government had agreed to recognize the court's jurisdiction in the case in hopes of improving its tarnished image internationally. In the end, more damaging than the guilty verdicts, which referred to violations during an earlier period, was the fact that two Honduran witnesses called to testify before the court—human rights activist Miguel Angel Pavón and police Sergeant José Isaias Vilorio—were assassinated in January 1988, allegedly by members of the Battalion 3/16, despite orders issued by the IACHR for the government to guarantee the protection of all witnesses. Similarly, although the government agreed to pay damages to the victims' families,[44] no military personnel were ever prosecuted for their role in the earlier abuses—in fact several officers singled out at the trial have subsequently been promoted—and the pattern of human rights violations has continued.

Acting with Impunity

"It would have been very good if instead of monetary compensation they could have brought the guilty to justice, put them in jail," Zenaida Velásquez responded to the IACHR's first verdict in the case of her "disappeared" brother Manfredo.[45] Angered by his September 1981 abduction, Zenaida helped found the Committee of Families of the Detained-Disappeared in Honduras (COFADEH), which has struggled through the Honduran court system for years.

The military's continued ability to act with impunity against its perceived political enemies underscores the incomplete nature of Honduras's shift to civilian rule. While the military touts its internal disciplinary process for demoting or discharging personnel involved in various crimes, at no time have soldiers or officers been tried in civilian courts for the political crimes defined as violations of human rights.

Following the ouster of General Alvarez in 1984, the armed forces announced their intention to launch an internal investigation into the abuses committed under his command. The long-awaited report, issued in 1985 in the form of a one-page communique, was a disappointment for many. "It was not possible to determine whether anyone in the military was connected with disappearances," was its chief conclusion.[46] When Alvarez himself returned from exile in April 1988, charges brought against him by COFADEH in the civilian courts were dropped when clerks lost the papers. Alvarez' successor, General Walter López, attempted to blame both the earlier and ongoing disappearances on supposed contra death squads.

The Honduran authorities have used other tactics in their efforts to deflect criticisms regarding human rights abuses. In 1988, for example, U.S. Methodist Minister Joe Eldridge, *New York Times* reporter James LeMoyne, and *Washington Post* reporter Julia Preston were all banned from the country after writing stories critical of the military and the human rights situation.[47]

The independent monitoring organization Committee for the Defense of Human Rights (CODEH) has been the target of ongoing harassment, including armed attacks on its offices, infiltration by government agents, repeated public death threats against its leaders, and the assassination of Miguel Angel Pavón, president of CODEH's San Pedro Sula chapter, in January 1988. While the government waged a campaign to portray Pavón's death as the result of an internal power struggle, a former member of Battalion 3/16 reported that his colleagues in the "death squad" were responsible for the killing. One U.S. embassy publication labels CODEH President Ramón Custodio as "a prominent Marxist ideologue," and State Department reports on human rights in Honduras dismiss many of the accusations made by CODEH and other independent monitoring groups as "politically motivated."[48]

The U.S. embassy and State Department have come under severe criticism from international human rights monitoring groups for their role in attempting to discredit organizations like CODEH whose work involves exposing and documenting abuses. Going one step further, Americas Watch has laid part of the blame for the rise in human rights violations on Washington: "Honduras is one of the countries that can most fairly be described as a U.S. client state, giving Washington a special responsibility to foster human rights improvement there. Yet U.S. behavior has fallen far short of the mark....The State Department still balks at acknowledgment of past crimes by the forces the United States trained."[49]

Attempts by family members of the victims of human rights abuses to bring the perpetrators to justice have been hampered by deficiencies and a lack of will in the country's justice system. The filing of writs of *habeas corpus* and other legal avenues rarely produce results. In part, the judicial system is paralyzed due to insufficient funding and the endemic corruption of the judges. According to the constitution, the judiciary is to receive 3 percent of the annual budget. But in 1986 and 1987 it received less than half that amount. The Honduran Minister of Justice admitted in 1988 that 84 percent of all inmates in the country's overcrowded prisons are simply being detained and only 16 percent have been convicted and sentenced.[50]

The government's own human rights watchdog, the Interagency Committee for Human Rights (COINDEH), is plagued by similar problems. Formed in June 1986, the group is composed of representatives from several state agencies and ministries who continue to be paid by their respective employers, plus four salaried investigators. In mid-1989 COINDEH was reportedly considering suspending its activities because it had still not received its budget allocations from the government.

The unabated pattern of human rights violations, compounded by the inefficiency of the judiciary system and COINDEH, have led Hondurans to form several independent organizations designed to pressure the government and military for greater respect of human rights. CODEH, formed in 1981, is the most active and prominent. With disappearances becoming commonplace in 1982, relatives of some of the victims formed the Committee of Families of the Detained-Disappeared (COFADEH). The group was instrumental in bringing the landmark IACHR case to trial in 1987. A women's group called Visitación Padilla has included the promotion of human rights as one of its main priorities.

Many had expected that growing popular pressures on the Azcona government, coupled with increased international scrutiny of Honduras in the wake of the Esquipulas accords and the IACHR verdicts in 1988-1989, would lead to a drop in human rights abuses as the 1980s drew to a close. But in practice, the trends established early in the decade continue. In its exhaustive survey of the May 1987-May 1989 period, Americas Watch concluded: "A steady succession of human rights abuses indicate deepening political violence and an erosion in respect for fundamental human rights....Killings of suspected common criminals by government forces are rife, and the discovery of bullet-ridden bodies on roadsides has become commonplace....Honduran authorities have demonstrated a lack of political will to find and punish the authors of these murders....Efforts to expose these abuses have met with steadfast opposition from the government and powerful military establishment."[51]

Chapter 2

Military

Security Forces

Following decades of intermittent direct rule by the armed forces, the army formally returned to its barracks in 1981. The deal to allow civilians to run the government turned out to be a good one for the armed forces. Behind the veneer of elected governments, and despite the fact that the country was neither at war nor facing an internal insurgency, the 1980s saw an unprecedented buildup of the Honduran armed forces. Between 1978 and 1984 U.S. military aid increased almost twenty-fold, while the armed forces doubled in size over the same period.[1] This buildup continued, albeit at a somewhat slower pace, throughout the decade.

Equally important as this quantitative expansion, during the 1980s the military consolidated its grip on the key levers of national policy formulation and decision-making.[2] As one observer put it, "the military has all the power and the civilians have all the problems."[3]

History and Structure of the Military

The history of the Honduran military as a professional standing force dates to 1954 when the United States concluded a Bilateral Military Assistance Treaty and sent Army and Air Force missions to train and equip their Honduran counterparts. Essentially the project sought to transform what had been a gendarme for U.S. fruit companies and the Honduran oligarchy into an autonomous, professional institution which would serve U.S. designs. On-site training and scholarships to U.S. military schools along with modest financial support characterized this relationship prior to the military expansion of the 1980s. (See U.S. Military Aid)

As is typical throughout Latin America, the military traditionally served as a police force to squelch worker and *campesino* unrest, usually on the basis of personal relations between a local barracks commander and the plantation or factory owner. In 1946 General Tiburcio Carías created a separate force to carry out that function, a body which would eventually evolve into the Public Security Force (FUSEP). It was from his position as chief of FUSEP that Colonel Gustavo Alvarez — with his special training in political repression that included military school in Argentina — rose to become commander in chief of the entire armed forces in 1982.

The armed forces are formally divided into four major service branches: the Army, the Air Force, the Naval Force, and the Public Security Force (FUSEP). Although the bulk of police and internal security functions reside with FUSEP and the police forces it controls, the Army has also been used extensively for these purposes. Estimates on the total number of full-time members of the combined armed forces range from 23,700 to 30,000.[4]

The Army expanded from a few thousand troops in the 1970s to an estimated 15,000 by 1989.[5] With the addition of two new brigades in early 1989, one artillery and one infantry, the Army now has five such units stationed around the country. Although much of Honduras is rugged, mountainous territory, the Army's arsenal includes some 90 tanks.[6] Among the different divisions of the armed forces, the Army has benefited the most from the over one hundred joint maneuvers held since the early 1980s with the United States. These maneuvers have worked primarily on the Honduran military's ability to perform together with U.S. troops and under U.S. command.

Led by a fleet of 37 combat jets out of a total fleet of 120 aircraft, the Honduran Air Force is considered the most powerful in Central America.[7] Washington's repeated stalling on delivery of a promised fleet of a dozen F-5 supersonic jet fighters — the first of which were delivered in December 1987 and the last in January 1990 — was a long-standing point of friction between the two countries. With a smaller and less combat-hardened Army than Guatemala, El Salvador and Nicaragua, and with a contra army almost as large as its own camped on its territory, Honduras regarded superiority in air power as indispensable. While other Central American countries have concentrated on using air power to support counterinsurgency efforts, the Honduran Air Force is equipped and trained for offensive operations against installations in other countries.

The Naval Force, which essentially functions as a coast guard, is small and equipped with only nine patrol boats. It is, however, the focus of increased attention under the aegis of the war on drugs.

FUSEP is controlled by army officers and is subordinated to the Ministry of Defense, although it has its own general staff and a separate organizational structure. In addition to its regular police units, FUSEP controls the treasury police, the traffic police, and a counterinsurgency unit known as the Cobras. The Honduran equivalent of the FBI, the National Investigations Division (DNI), formed in 1976, is also formally under the control of FUSEP. The DNI carries out routine criminal detective work, as well as surveillance and intelligence operations. In total, there are some 4,500 members of the various police forces controlled by FUSEP.[8] In 1987 the Reagan administration circumvented a congressional ban on police aid by redirecting military assistance to FUSEP under the State Department's Anti-Terrorist Program. The assistance took the form of a massive infusion of guns and communications equipment, as well as a small amount for human rights training.

The intelligence section of the armed forces, known as the G-2 and functioning under the command of the Joint Chiefs of Staff, is primarily responsible for keeping tabs on political opponents and military personnel. This secret police unit created and operates Battalion 3/16 — the official death squad — and carries out propaganda campaigns against domestic opposition groups, critics and dissenters. While Battalion 3/16 is directed by intelligence officers, it recruits its operatives from numerous forces such as FUSEP, the DNI, and the immigration service. The operatives remain at their jobs as cover to restrict knowledge of the unit's existence even within the military institution.

Outside the military's major service branches, the armed forces also control several additional institutions. Most important are the dozens of military academies and schools spread around the country for the training of both recruits and officers. The Logistical Support Center is responsible for the storage and transportation of materials and equipment and constituted a key liaison for arms deliveries to the contras between 1982 and 1987. Active duty armed forces personnel are complemented with standby and general reserve groups. The armed forces have their own office for administration of a military pension fund, as well as their own nationally chartered bank.

In all branches of the military, officers tend to come from the middle classes and enter the military from academies rather than by rising through the ranks. As a result, rivalries and divisions within the armed forces tend to follow the lines of shared "promotions" or graduating classes more than political or ideological factors. Outside the officer corps, voluntary enlistment is rare and the military relies on crude methods of forced recruitment to press poor youths into service.

For those who enter as officers, the military is an important mechanism for social climbing. The privileges that officer status provides, along with opportunities for graft and corruption, have resulted in quick and dramatic fortunes. Numerous Honduran officers are beginning to acquire land and enter agroexport industries, both through illicit appropriation of state lands, and as gifts received from grateful landowners.[9] Although still not on the scale seen, for example, in Guatemala, links between the military and the oligarchy are growing and the armed forces now control insurance and investment companies as well as a bank.

The military's direct participation in contra supply transactions, and alleged large-scale involvement in drug trafficking among some high-ranking officials, richly compliment other less criminal avenues for moneymaking.[10] Although much of the military buildup of the 1980s was bankrolled through the U.S. military-assistance program (See U.S. Military Aid), defense spending consistently ate up between 20 and 30 percent of the national budget.[11]

National Security Doctrine and Militarization

In Honduras, the process of militarization — defined not as the quantitative buildup of the armed forces and its weaponry but as the encroachment of military practices and control on civil daily life — stretches back many years.[12] The Constitution of 1957 eliminated civilian authority over the military, transferring ultimate control of the institution to the chief of the armed forces who was given the right to disobey presidential orders that he considered unconstitutional.

This formal authority provided a legal basis for the political independence and autonomous institutional development of the military and set the stage for its subsequent incursions into all areas of national affairs. This process has been facilitated by the traditional atomization and weakness of the Honduran political parties, state, and oligarchy. In much of the countryside, local military commanders wield more influence than civilian authorities. In many remote areas the army is the only representative of the central government. At the national level the military established itself as the ultimate arbiter of disputes between rival political, social, and economic forces.

Shaken by its poor performance in the brief war with El Salvador in 1969, the military embarked upon a project of expansion with better training and more sophisticated weaponry, broadening its mandate to include defense against foreign threats to national sovereignty. The revolutionary upsurges in Central America in the late 1970s — and particularly the Sandinista victory in Nicaragua — together with the staging-ground role chosen for Honduras by the Carter administration, thrust the militarization process into high gear.

The chief Honduran architect of this process was General Gustavo Alvarez, whose tenure at the head of the armed forces officially lasted from January 1982 until March 1984. According to one analyst of Honduran affairs, "Alvarez was arguably the first Honduran leader to have a coherent project for his country, based on the doctrine of national security, and the capacity to implement it."[13] The traditional Latin American versions of national-security doctrine, developed and applied by the military dictatorships of Argentina and Brazil in the 1960s and 1970s, see the world as a rigid, bipolar battleground where the forces of international communism are engaged in a permanent struggle to subvert the western democracies. Subversives are often defined as all those who are opposed to the government and the military is seen as above scrutiny by civilian authorities.

Alvarez was guided by the principles of the national-security doctrine, to which he was exposed during extensive training in Argentina, and through the Argentine military advisers he brought in to work with Honduran officers. From his post as Commander in Chief of the Armed Forces, Alvarez initiated a process of militarization which would continue unabated throughout the decade, introducing profound changes in Honduran society and politics along the way. In essence, the Honduran conception of national-security doctrine entails the substitution of traditional notions of geographical and territorial enemies and borders for ideological ones. As such, the armed forces' mandate to provide territorial defense against enemy armies, particularly the Salvadoran, was subordinated to a new project of ideological defense against "subversion and communism."

Internally this meant engaging in a "preventive" war against the nascent Honduran revolutionary left, popular organizations, and in the extreme, anyone considered "potentially subversive" by the security forces. According to Honduran analysts, "Here national-security doctrine implies the elimination of all those considered to be socially dysfunctional. In other words, both common criminals and political dissidents are subject to physical elimination."[14] In the international realm it meant collaborating with the United States in its contra war against Nicaragua and with the Salvadoran armed forces against the FMLN.

Concretely, the military defined its defense posture for the 1980s on the basis of three distinct scenarios:

* **Internal preventive warfare against "subversion:"** This required the geographical dispersion of troops throughout national territory; ample training in counterinsurgency techniques; a greater role in

intelligence gathering and processing; and participation in
civic-action programs and joint maneuvers with U.S. forces.

* **Containment of revolutionary forces in Central America:** This
implied collaboration with the counterinsurgency efforts of the
Salvadoran and Guatemalan military and with U.S. efforts to
overthrow the Sandinista government chiefly through rearguard
support for the contras; and the construction of military
installations capable of handling a large-scale deployment of U.S.
forces.

* **Conventional territorial defense:** While the unresolved border
dispute with El Salvador has taken a back seat to other priorities, it
has by no means disappeared and the armed forces continue to
foster specific elements of the military buildup with a view towards
the possibility of fighting a conventional war.

Some of the infrastructure necessary for waging General Alvarez'
proclaimed "war to the death against internal subversion and communism
in Central America" was already in place. Nonetheless, a series of institutions and procedures were set up in the early 1980s to streamline the
process and to allow it to be carried out behind the veneer of an elected
civilian government:

* **Battalion 3/16:** A clandestine paramilitary structure created by
Alvarez in 1980 while he was head of FUSEP, Battalion 3/16 is
referred to as the Honduran "death squad." It has been singled out
by defectors from among its ranks and by Honduran human rights
organizations as the key unit responsible for the disappearance and
extrajudicial execution of hundreds of Honduran civilians. (See
Human Rights)

* **Cobras:** This elite counterinsurgency battalion was created as part
of FUSEP in 1979 and upgraded with better weaponry and training
under the command of General Alvarez in the early 1980s. It has
been used to repress activities by labor unions and against guerrilla
groups.

* **National Defense and Security Council (CSN):** Created by the 1982
Constitution and modeled after the U.S. National Security Council,
the CSN is composed of ten of the nation's top leaders, six from the
military and four civilians. While the council functions without any
legal or regulatory framework and its deliberations are secret, it has
been defined as a "suprapower" responsible for approving the
broad contours of national policy, particularly in the strategic areas
of security and foreign relations.[15]

* **Anti-terrorist legislation:** In April 1982 the Honduran Congress passed legislation stipulating jail sentences of 20 years and up for "subversion," defined to include traditional forms of protest used by popular organizations and unions, such as land takeovers, factory occupations and street demonstrations. Although the anti-terrorist decree was subsequently abolished, its most repressive articles were incorporated into the country's new penal code included legal punishments for a series of activities defined as "terrorism."[16]

* **Civil Defense Committees (CDC):** Modeled after the Salvadoran paramilitary organization called ORDEN, the CDCs were designed as civilian vigilante groups charged with reporting "unusual activities" in their communities and villages to the police or military.

* **Center for Emergency Information (CIE):** A national, 24-hour telephone hotline set up by FUSEP in September 1983 for anonymous "denunciations of suspicious acts against the security of persons and institutions of the state."[17]

* **Military treaties with the United States:** In 1954 the United States and Honduras signed a Bilateral Military Assistance Treaty to regulate military relations between the two countries. In 1982 General Alvarez initiated lengthy negotiations with the Pentagon over additional protocols to the 1954 treaty which would facilitate the large-scale expansion of U.S. military installations in Honduras and provide a veil of legality to the occupation of the country by U.S. forces.

* **APROH:** In January 1983 a group of leading businessmen and rightwing politicians formed the Association for the Progress of Honduras. With General Alvarez as president, APROH attempted to mobilize sectors of civil society behind the national-security project and to coordinate the economic aspects of the plan. In the words of APROH executive secretary Benjamín Villanueva — Treasury Minister in the Callejas government — "APROH's objective is to fight Marxism with ideas. Alvarez does it in other ways."[18]

The Rise and Fall of Alvarez

General Alvarez was the key engineer of the National Security Doctrine in Honduras.[19] From his position as colonel at the head of FUSEP and the DNI in 1980, Alvarez — a staunch anticommunist and close ally of the United States — experienced a swift and dramatic rise to the heights of power in Honduras. In early 1982 Alvarez was named head of the Superior Council of the Armed Forces (COSUFFAA), the group of top officers responsible for defining military policy. In April of that year, newly elected Liberal Party President Suazo Córdova, a close personal friend of Alvarez, violated long-standing military norms and procedures to ensure the promotion of Alvarez to Brigadier General.

Alvarez quickly consolidated his hold on power by dispatching his two main rivals, Colonel Leonidas Torres Arias and Colonel Hubbert Bodden, to diplomatic exile in Argentina and Taiwan. Finally, in November 1982, Alvarez forced through a series of constitutional amendments under which the role of Commander in Chief was transferred to himself, as head of the armed forces, while the president, who had formerly enjoyed that position, was instead given the ceremonial title of Supreme Chief. The country has long had a cabinet-level post of Minister of Defense, but unlike others in Latin America, in Honduras it is a bureaucratic position with little authority and in any case is always awarded to a military officer, not a civilian.

The general's close relations with Suazo, and with newly arrived U.S. ambassador John Negroponte, allowed the three to form a powerful triumvirate which would transform the face of the country in the short space of two years. In 1982 Honduras became the second-largest recipient of U.S. military aid in Latin America. The $31.3 million it received in that year almost surpassed the total in military aid for the entire 1946-1981 period ($32.5 million). In May 1982 Alvarez negotiated an amendment to the 1954 bilateral military agreement between Honduras and the United States, paving the way for an unprecedented string of joint military maneuvers (an estimated 70 were held between 1982-1989) and the rapid improvement in Honduras' military infrastructure. New military construction during this period included dozens of airstrips, communications and radar facilities, tank traps, and port facilities.

The Honduran armed forces' earlier focus on collaborative efforts with the Salvadoran army against the FMLN, though never dropped, was replaced with all out efforts to assist the Nicaraguan counterrevolution in its war against the Sandinistas.[20] Finally, Alvarez presided over the rapid escalation in human rights violations as the national-security apparatus set out to decapitate the incipient revolutionary organizations and stifle popular discontent over the economic crisis, growing militarization and involvement of the country in regional conflicts. (See Human Rights)

Alvarez eventually became the victim of his own excesses and was ousted in a March 1984 coup by rival military officers led by air force commander General Walter López. Fueled by nationalist sentiments, discontent in the officers corps had been brewing for months over issues such as Alvarez' reckless plans to invade Nicaragua, his all-too-cozy relations with the traditionally adversarial Salvadoran military, and the negative repercussions on the armed forces' image caused by his massive and open support for the contras and disdain for human rights. Furthermore, many officers resented the fact that Honduras was receiving far too little from Washington in exchange for the strategic role the country was playing in U.S. regional policy.

But above all, it was the thirst for absolute power which led to the downfall of Alvarez. In early March, when he attempted to reduce COSUFFAA from 52 to 21 members, restrict its mandate, and virtually replace it with an eight-member Commanders Junta loyal to himself, the coup plotters moved into action.

The new military leaders did manage to institute some changes. COSUFFAA norms and procedures, widely ignored by Alvarez, were reinstated. In May, they initiated a prolonged process of negotiations with Washington aimed at modifying the 1954 agreement and assuring both a greater say for Honduras in bilateral affairs and increased aid levels. In June 1985 the controversial Regional Military Training Center (CREM), installed by the United States under Alvarez to train Salvadoran troops, was officially closed down. Although the fundamental relationship with the contras remained the same, the military did force them to take a lower profile, confining them to their camps along the border, and began insisting on commitments from Washington to take ultimate responsibly should they be defeated by the Nicaraguan army.

Attempts were also made to improve the military's human rights image by publicly denouncing certain abuses, occasionally agreeing to meet with human rights advocates, and setting up a special committee to investigate past abuses. But the changes were only cosmetic. While the death squads were reined in, none of the repressive structures erected under Alvarez were dismantled, and indeed disappearances, illegal detentions, and assassinations continued much as before. The military attempted to deflect criticism by publicly accusing the contras for such abuses. Likewise, the U.S. maneuvers and military buildup continued apace.

Colonel Efraín González, head of the armed forces high command, underscored the extent to which the key elements of the strategy and infrastructure set up by Alvarez, Negroponte, and Suazo would live on despite Alvarez' departure: "It is important to note that in the armed forces high command there has been no philosophical change. There is no different ideological or political attitude, but rather a new military structure to attempt to do things in a more correct manner..."[21]

Inside the military, the net effect of the 1984 coup was the diffusion of authority which had been concentrated in Alvarez' hands across a broader spectrum of officers, ranging from the younger, more nationalist-minded ones, to more traditional rightwing sectors. For a brief period, the former began to exert pressures for substantive changes in the military's behavior. But in February 1986 armed forces chief General Walter López, the de facto leader of this group, was forced to resign, replaced by the hard-line former Navy commander General Humberto Regalado.

Under Regalado the military returned to more amicable and subservient relations with the United States and generally deepened its activities aimed at squelching internal unrest and popular protest with a consequent rise in human rights abuses.[22] Some of the repressive structures which had lain dormant since the departure of Alvarez were reactivated, and some new ones created. The military placed a new emphasis on civic-action programs chiefly aimed at creating an image of benevolence for the armed forces among the population. And the army acted, mostly through the media, to portray political opponents and dissidents as common criminals and delinquents.

Amidst nagging accusations of corruption, and despite efforts to prolong his presence in the post, Regalado was forced to step down as military leader in late 1989. Regalado, who belongs to the group of officers known as the Fifth Promotion, was replaced by his hand-picked successor, Colonel Arnulfo Cantarero López from the Sixth Promotion. Although the U.S.-trained colonel has served in the military for 26 years, Cantarero is not seen as a powerful leader. He has held only two top leadership positions in the past, both in the armed forces weakest branch, the Naval Forces. Many see Cantarero's nomination as a compromise to avoid further divisions or infighting within the armed forces high command over the promotion of more influential individuals.[23]

By the late 1980s opposition to ongoing militarization had reached beyond the popular sectors and into the civilian elite. Fearful that the very project designed to assure stability in Honduras was in fact contributing to the opposite, they expressed their concerns with growing frankness. "There is a feeling here that if we don't do things the way the military establishment wants, we will have a coup," complained Jaime Rosenthal, an influential businessman and one of Azcona's vice presidents. "But for me, the real issue is not how strong we are militarily. If we cannot show that our system is better than Nicaragua's, that our standard of living is higher, no army will be able to contain the desire of our people to adopt the Nicaraguan system."[24]

Paramilitary Groups

Most analysts agree that Honduras does not have paramilitary groups in the sense of organizations truly separate of and independent from the armed forces. The bulk of the evidence relating to human rights violations shows that units which belong or are closely linked to the military carry out the political abduction and murders, and systematically use torture on common as well as political prisoners. In general, use of the term "death squad" in the Honduran context is an attempt to distract attention from the military's systematic extra-legal use of force in countering a broad range of perceived threats to national security.

The military, for its part, usually denies formal involvement with any of these groups. One exception is the Battalion 3/16, the group most often referred to as a Honduran death squad.[25] (See Security Forces) Formed under the jurisdiction of the intelligence branch of the Honduran military during the rule of General Alvarez, Battalion 3/16 has been accused by human rights monitoring organizations as the main group responsible for the wave of disappearances and extrajudicial killings which took place in the early 1980s. (See Human Rights) On the heels of intense negative publicity, the military announced that the unit had been "permanently recessed" in September 1987. Nonetheless, declarations given by deserters from the ranks of Battalion 3/16, and other piecemeal evidence, suggests that the unit has actually been reorganized and given a lower profile, while continuing to carry out its work much as before.[26]

Three additional groups are shrouded in even more secrecy and controversy: the Anticommunist Action Alliance (AAA), the Free Honduras Movement, and the Honduran Committee for Peace and Democracy. Most active of the three is the AAA, which also made its appearance under Alvarez. After several years of inactivity, the AAA resurfaced in April 1988 following a wave of anti-U.S. demonstrations and the subsequent crackdown by the military. At that time, it distributed thousands of flyers bearing the names and photographs of 22 persons said to be "poisoning the ideological spirit of Honduran youth." The list included national leaders from student groups, unions, and human rights organizations.[27] In January 1989 the AAA took out paid advertisements on several television and radio stations vowing to kill five prominent Hondurans in retribution for the killing of General Alvarez earlier that month.[28]

The human rights group CODEH refers to these groups as "ghost organizations" whose activities are actually sponsored by the Military Technical Projects (PROMITEC), a unit run by the Armed Forces General

Staff which specializes in psychological warfare. The human rights group says it has documentary evidence linking the AAA to the military.[29]

Substantive evidence has never been provided for the military's assertion that all disappearances and political assassinations in Honduras are the work of the contras. Nonetheless reports indicate that the contras have used their own paramilitary squads not only against defectors from their own ranks, but against Hondurans as well.

While paramilitary activity mushroomed during the reign of Alvarez, its immediate roots trace back to the period prior to his rise to prominence. Within months of the 1979 Sandinista victory in Nicaragua three previously unknown groups appeared in Honduras publicly threatening to assassinate popular organization and leftist leaders: the National Front for the Defense of Democracy, the Honduran Anti-Communist Movement (MACHO) and the Anti-Communist Combat Army (ELA). Subsequent reports indicated that all three groups were working under the auspices of FUSEP.[30]

Guerrilla Groups

Despite the existence of conditions similar to those which gave rise to the revolutionary left in neighboring El Salvador and Guatemala, Honduras has never confronted a sustained challenge from a guerrilla insurgency. In part, this is due to the success of the relatively sophisticated and intensive repression carried out in the early 1980s, which decapitated the leftwing organizations through assassinations, disappearances, and exile. Others point to the left's inability to present a coherent alternative capable of capitalizing on widespread popular discontent, as well as the Honduran state's strategy of cooptation and the use of limited reforms aimed at neutralizing the influence of progressive individuals and organizations.

While guerrilla groups have claimed responsibility for many of the bombings and armed attacks against U.S. military personnel which have taken place since 1981, at least some of these appear to be the work of the Honduran military itself.[31] In March 1989 several leaders of the Honduran popular movement publicly asserted that the military was behind a recent series of bombings and death threats which they called part of a "psychological war which seeks to create panic and justify repression against those who defend Honduran sovereignty, peace, and human rights."[32] Others cite accounts linking the military to incidents such as the bombing of a Peace Corps office and the San Pedro Sula shooting of several U.S. soldiers, both in 1988, as evidence of growing antagonism among members of the armed forces towards the United States.[33]

In the absence of a revolutionary alternative, a revised leftist agenda has been taken up by social and popular organizations including the FUTH labor federation, the CNTC peasant league, the COLPRO-SUMAH teachers union, and the Honduran Patriotic Front (FPH), as well as several secondary and university student groups.

Most of the left's leaders who managed to escape the repression of the early 1980s fled into exile. In June of 1983 five of the remaining guerrilla groups announced the formation of an alliance called the National Unitary Direction of the Honduran Revolutionary Movement (DNUMRH). Most of the groups emerged in the late 1970s as offshoots of the Honduran Communist Party (PCH), the Marxist-Leninist splinter group (PCH-ML), or from radical student groups. The DNU includes:[34]

* **Cinchoneros Popular Liberation Movement (MPL):** Named after a 19th-century peasant leader, the Cinchoneros was formed by university student leaders in 1980. The group came to prominence in 1981 and 1982 when it took responsibility for an airline hijacking and the holding of a number of hostages in the San Pedro Sula Chamber of Commerce. A communique signed by the Cinchoneros claimed responsibility for the January 1989 killing of General Alvarez, although other sources maintain that the military itself carried out the action fearing that a repentant Alvarez, a born-again Christian, might denounce his former allies.[35]

* **Morazanist Front for the Liberation of Honduras (FMLNH):** The Front is the armed wing of the PCH-ML. It has claimed responsibility for at least five armed attacks against U.S. military personnel stationed in Honduras in which 22 U.S. soldiers were wounded.[36]

* **Revolutionary Party of Central American Workers (PRTC-H):** In July of 1983 a hundred-man column of the PRTC infiltrated the jungles of southern Honduras and attempted to establish a presence there. Within two months, most of the group, including its leader José María Reyes Matta and a U.S. priest, Father James Guadalupe Carney, had been killed in a massive counteroffensive launched by the army's elite Cobra forces under the guidance of U.S. counterinsurgency experts.[37]

* **Lorenzo Zelaya Popular Revolutionary Forces (FPR):** Also formed by university students, the FPR is named after a 1960s peasant

leader who headed an attempt to establish a guerrilla front in the mountains of Yoro before being crushed by the army.

Since the August 1987 signing of the Esquipulas II Peace Accords, the DNU and some of its member groups have issued public proposals regarding potential agenda items for a national dialogue and calling for their inclusion on the National Reconciliation Commission. In a surprising move, in June 1989 armed forces chief Humberto Regalado called for the inclusion of the guerrillas in an upcoming national dialogue meeting. Although the DNU issued a communique accepting the invitation, the proposal was subsequently dropped.[38]

Although polarization and social hardships in Honduras are likely to deepen under the administration of National Party President Callejas, the omnipotence of the Honduran and U.S. military and intelligence networks make the appearance of an armed revolutionary movement unlikely in the coming years.

Chapter 3

Economy

State of the Economy

In a region known for its poverty and underdevelopment, Honduras has traditionally been the poorest and least developed. The country's agrarian-based economy is highly dependent on export earnings from a few crops and on the handful of foreign companies which dominate productive activity. Meanwhile, most Hondurans continue to survive as subsistence farmers living largely outside the market economy.

The last 30 years have brought many changes in the Honduran economy. Successive governments over this period have introduced reforms and policies aimed at modernizing the economy and putting it on the path to more sustainable growth. More recently, Washington pushed a new export-led private-sector development strategy, heavily dependent on foreign investment, in the hope of transforming Honduras into a show-case for free-market capitalism. The growth model Honduras has embraced has not generated significant internal development, but has led to increased foreign domination of the economy and has exacerbated existing inequalities among the population.

Underdevelopment and Modernization

Unlike Guatemala and El Salvador, Honduras never developed a powerful agroexport-based oligarchy with the attendant extremes of wealth and poverty. Lacking rich volcanic soils and a large indigenous population to exploit as cheap labor, the country remained a backwater throughout the first half of the 1900s. This historical lack of economic dynamism helped Honduras avoid the stark inequalities, polarization, and social upheavals which characterize its neighbors.

In the absence of a strong national economy and a cohesive economic elite, Honduras was little more than a "banana republic" for most of this century. The country's politics and economy were dominated by foreign fruit and mining companies. Outside the banana enclaves of the North Coast and scattered mining centers, the economy mostly consisted of a large peasantry engaged in subsistence agriculture, a small group of private ranchers, and a tiny urban commercial sector.

It was not until the 1950s and 1960s that the country's larger land-owners and its emerging business class began to organize in an attempt to chart a new course of economic growth for Honduras. First to organize were the country's conservative cattle ranchers and large estate owners who in the 1950s banded together to form the National Association of Growers and Cattlemen (FENAGH). A decade later the country's emerging business class formed its own association called the Honduran Private Enterprise Council (COHEP).

The initial goal of economic modernization was to expand commercial agricultural production beyond the banana plantations through the introduction of other export crops such as coffee, cotton and sugar. Later, in the 1960s and 1970s, Honduras began to pursue an import-substitution industrialization strategy, becoming a partner in the newly created Central American Common Market (CACM). These initial modernization strategies brought mixed, though largely disappointing results. Other agricultural products, particularly coffee and beef exports, did take hold and provided the basis for limited national development. Nonetheless, to this day bananas continue to generate the bulk of export earnings. Honduran industries did develop but proved unable to compete with the industrial sectors of its neighbors. The 1969 border war with El Salvador and the subsequent deterioration of CACM further undermined plans for industrial growth.

The continued domination of foreign investors also limited the benefits of economic modernization. The transnational banana corporations, for example, led much of the diversification into new agricultural products like citrus and African palm. These same banana giants also opened food-processing industries.

Part of the modernization strategy in the 1960s and 1970s was dependent upon a new, more aggressive role for the state. A host of new state and parastatal agencies took an active role in agriculture, banking, and labor. The elaborate state-sponsored network, however, turned out to be more effective as a breeding ground for inefficiency and corruption than as a promoter of development. Public expenditures mushroomed as private-sector elites took advantage of generous subsidies and loans. But rather than using the money for investment and development projects, they used it for ongoing operations, shifting their capital into more profitable ventures or foreign bank accounts.[1]

Crisis of the Eighties

Between 1960 and 1980 Honduras experienced average annual growth rates of over 5 percent. But declining terms of trade, the slump in the international economy, and growing foreign debt and budget deficits contributed to a major recession in the early 1980s. These factors, combined with an inefficient industrial sector and an agricultural sector still dependent on banana exports, crushed hopes for economic modernization.

The short-term "solution" was a massive influx of foreign aid coupled with limited austerity measures. For the long term, Honduras adopted the U.S.-designed process of orienting its economy towards a greater reliance on internationally competitive nontraditional exports. An "export boom" was to be generated by new investments in enterprises in both agriculture and industry, and by the privatization of many of the state-run companies.

The results of these new diversification and privatization plans have not been propitious thus far. Rarely in the 1980s have economic growth rates equaled the country's per capita growth. At the end of the decade declining export earnings, rising inflation, and diminishing foreign-exchange revenues put the economy into a serious slump. Even if the economy recovers, extraordinarily strong and sustained growth will be necessary to remedy the economic ills that plague the Honduran economy as it enters the 1990s:

* **Shortages of foreign exchange reserves:** By the late 1980s the country had barely enough reserves to cover one month's worth of imports, leading to de facto import restrictions, drops in production dependent upon imported materials, and spot shortages of essential goods. The currency shortage has been aggravated by a credit freeze and cutoff of new loans from the IMF and World Bank because of debt arrearages and failure to fully implement recommended structural-adjustment measures.

* **Chronic trade deficit:** Honduras suffers from a chronic trade deficit, having run a trade surplus (exports over imports) in only three of the last 30 years. Despite measures taken to boost exports, the country's large trade gap did not narrow significantly over the course of the 1980s.

* **Lack of foreign and national investment:** Despite the abundance of special privileges and incentives aimed at stimulating new export ventures, the negligible rate of foreign and national investment in the 1980s has not kept pace with factory closings and the estimated half a billion dollars in capital flight.[2] In fact, domestic private

investment declined 67 percent from 1980-1985.[3] One survey of the investment climate in 112 countries ranked Honduras number 94.[4]

* **Rising foreign debt:** Foreign debt, which has doubled since 1981, stood at $3.4 billion in 1989 and debt service payments amounted to an average of almost $1 million a day. The government ceased payments on most of its debt commitments arguing that it is simply unable to pay. Honduras has one of the lowest credit ratings in the world.

* **Uncontrolled fiscal deficit:** Throughout the 1980s factors like debt service payments, massive public spending, and growing military expenditures contributed to a growing fiscal deficit. Although it has been narrowed somewhat in the last few years, the government's fiscal deficit remains unmanageably large at nearly 10 percent of GDP.

Structural tendencies tell only one part of the economic story. The austerity measures implemented to correct macroeconomic distortions, together with an export promotion strategy which chiefly benefits foreign companies and a tiny Honduran business elite, have taken a heavy toll on the majority of Hondurans. The principal trends afflicting Hondurans at the end of the 1980s were:

* **Increasing poverty:** The number of Hondurans living in poverty has risen to an alarming 68 percent of the population, 56 percent whom cannot even cover basic food needs.[5] According to the World Health Organization, three of every four Hondurans suffers from some degree of malnutrition.[6]

* **Rising unemployment:** Official unemployment was 12 percent in 1988 but estimates of combined un and underemployment run as high as 70 percent of the economically active population. Only one in ten Hondurans holds a steady job.

* **Declining wages:** Although annual inflation has been kept under 10 percent, purchasing power of wage earners dropped sharply over the last ten years. Average real wages have fallen every year since 1981.[7]

* **Increasing income inequalities:** Prior to the onset of the economic crisis of the 1980s, which clearly exacerbated existing income inequalities, the wealthiest 20 percent of the Honduran population received nearly 60 percent of all income, while the poorest 20 percent subsisted on just 4 percent of national income.[8]

Nontraditionals and Privatization

To some extent, the strategies ostensibly designed to pull Honduras out of its misery only serve to exacerbate existing problems of poverty and inequality. Most of the profits generated by the ambitious export strategies of the 1980s remained in the hands of the foreign companies which continue to dominate the economy, or go to the handful of Honduran entrepreneurs who have been willing to take the investment risks.

A case in point is the ambitious program of nontraditional exports — including items such as melons, cucumbers, cigars, cardamom, jam, and softballs — pursued throughout the decade. Several laws passed in the 1980s designed to stimulate investments in export projects, particularly in nontraditionals, provide exemptions from duties and tariffs on imported goods, tax reductions on exports, and in some cases an exemption for up to ten years on all taxes derived from profits on exports. In an effort to streamline the cumbersome bureaucratic procedures formerly constraining exports, the Ministry of Economy set up a one-stop export office where all requirements are centralized.

Although these generous incentives did spark some advances, the overall performance of the nontraditionals has been far below the early expectations. In fact, between 1980 and 1986 revenues from nontraditionals exports steadily declined in relation to income from traditional exports like bananas and coffee.[9] Perhaps more important, the ultimate effect of the growth in this sector has been to reinforce existing inequalities. Seen as high-risk due to rapid fluctuations in international market prices, nontraditionals have tended to reinforce the power of the small group of modern agroexport producers, further marginalizing the majority of Honduran *campesinos* from the market economy.

The growing trend of privatization — spurred by passage of a privatization law by Congress in early 1989 — also stands to disproportionately benefit foreign investors. By 1990 ten state businesses worth about $27 million had been sold to private investors[10] and another 47 companies, including those linked to CONADI and COHDEFOR, were up for sale. Observers noted that the majority will wind up in foreign hands as few Honduran entrepreneurs have the capital necessary to buy or operate them, and the handful who do have access to sufficient capital are unlikely to make risky investments.[11]

Many companies will be sold to foreign enterprises at a fraction of their market value to cover debts. In 1989, for example, debt-equity swaps financed the takeover of an abandoned paper plant by the Costa Rican-based company Scott Paper, while the Nelsin Group of Seattle bought a foundry and Wellington Hall purchased a furniture factory. The government is currently looking for buyers for the national airline, SAHSA, and COHEP has called for privatization of services including water, electricity, and communications.

The most pressing short-term problem for the new Callejas government was the shortage of foreign exchange reserves. In the long term, the only way for the new government to overcome the liquidity crisis was to negotiate a new agreement with the IMF to free up loans, credits, and assistance from the U.S. Agency for International Development (AID) and international lending institutions. Callejas implemented a package of structural-adjustment measures in March 1990 aimed at paving the way for negotiations on such an agreemnt.

Without taking the dive into full-scale currency devaluation, Callejas moved in that direction by legalizing the parallel exchange market (black market) for all transactions except payments on the foreign debt. Other aspects of Callejas' economic plan included tax hikes on sales, leases, imports, exports, and fuel; the elimination of some tax exemptions and privileges for diplomatic missions, nongovernmental organizations (NGOs), the armed forces, cooperatives, and unions; additional export incentives, and the reduction or abolition of protectionist tariffs.

The Callejas administration's ambitious plans for reviving the Honduran economy through privatization and export promotion are sure to face many challenges. Among them will be maintaining a minimum of social peace while implementing the austerity measures demanded by the IMF. A related problem will be how to attract foreign capital, both loans and investment, into risky Honduras in an increasingly competitive international environment. Finally, for any long-term success, the government will have to create conditions which will entice investments from the historically risk-shy Honduran private sector.

Agriculture

As in most of Central America, the agricultural sector in Honduras is the single most important contributor to the GDP, as well as to export earnings and employment.[12] Although hard times for farmers have induced steady rural-urban migration during the 1980s, the majority of the population still lives in the countryside.[13]

Overall, Honduras enjoys a relatively low population density but this is deceptive as only about one-fifth of the country's land is suitable for agriculture. The bulk of the good land—generally, the fertile low-lying valleys and coastal plains—is owned by large Honduran agroexport farmers or transnational companies. Food for local consumption is generally produced by peasants with small plots of lower quality land, usually on marginal steep and rocky mountainsides. The agricultural sector generally is characterized by low yields owing to inefficiencies at all levels. Only one in five farms in Honduras is worked by its owner; the rest are exploited under a variety of regimes from sharecropping, tenant farmers and squatters, to the traditional *ejido*, or municipal lands.[14]

Although the concentration of land and wealth is less extreme than in neighboring Guatemala and El Salvador, both land ownership and rural income are highly skewed in Honduras. Approximately half of the rural population is considered essentially landless, while many of those who do own lands are living on plots too small and of too poor quality even to meet subsistence needs. A full 55 percent of the farming population work plots smaller than five acres generating a net per capita income of less than $70 a year. At the other extreme, a mere 510 people own farms larger than 1700 acres with a corresponding per capita income of almost $15,000.[15] Some 60 percent of all the country's arable land is in the hands of the government and the two main transnationals, United Brands and Castle & Cooke.[16]

Agroexport Production

Honduran agricultural exports remained fairly steady throughout the 1980s. Bananas provided more than one-third of the country's total export revenues, followed by coffee which accounted for approximately one-fifth. The next three most important items — wood, beef, and seafood — each contributed less than 5 percent of export earnings. Honduras continues to be one of the largest exporters of bananas in the world, with "yellow gold" accounting for a whopping 44 percent of the country's agricultural export earnings in 1987.[17]

Since the early 1900s bananas have been the country's chief export item. Few of the profits, however, remain in Honduran hands as the transnational companies maintain control over commercialization of the fruit which is where most profits are generated. According to one study, only 16 percent of the profits from the production and sale of bananas remain in the hands of the producer countries.[18] In 1989 Honduras withdrew from UPEB, the cartel of banana-exporting countries, reportedly acceding to heavy pressure by the banana transnationals.[19] Production of bananas in Honduras takes place mostly on the lowlands of the North Coast.

Unlike bananas, production of and income from coffee remain in Honduran hands and most of the country's 45,000 producers are small growers. Although coffee has played an important role as a source of employment and has been prioritized as an alternative to dependence on bananas, minimal levels of technical assistance and credit contribute to Honduras having the lowest productivity and average yields in the region. Fluctuating international market prices and unfavorable export quotas have made coffee production increasingly risky. Export revenues have fallen each year since 1986 despite increased volumes.

Beef production has also dropped off in large part due to low world market prices. For the most part, cattle raising is carried out in traditional fashion, dependent on rain and grass pasture, resulting in low yields. Most ranching in Honduras is in the hands of a small group of powerful landowners who use over 25 percent of Honduras' agricultural land, including the best farmlands, thereby excluding more productive use of this land.

Seafood holds the promise of becoming one of Honduras' most lucrative agro-industries. Export earnings from fishing—mainly shrimp and lobster—are substantial and growing. The best prospects lie in shrimp farming. Cultivated shrimp earnings reached $19 million in 1988 and, with heavy investments underway, are expected to climb rapidly in the coming years. Most shrimp farming takes place in the Gulf of Fonseca, which borders on Nicaragua and El Salvador. Most of the foreign investments have come from the United States, Ecuador, and Taiwan. Attempts have been made to get small farmers into the shrimp-cultivation business, but large-scale, high-tech projects predominate. One such project is being carried out on the North Coast as part of a larger debt-equity swap between Chase Manhattan Bank and the Honduran government.[20]

Part of the effort to break dependency on the long-standing big earners like bananas and coffee has been the promotion of nontraditional exports. In agriculture, these include goods such as pineapples, melons, cucumbers, cardamom, black pepper, and ornamental flowers. Although some of the new projects have fared well, others have proved a dismal failure.

Food Security

The other side of the agroexport push is the declining per capita production of basic grains and increased food imports.[21] Although the agricultural sector as a whole has experienced moderate growth since 1984, consumers have faced growing shortages of staples like meat, corn, milk, chicken, eggs, and sugar.[22] Honduras, which was once self-sufficient in food production, is now forced to import basic foodstuffs each year. Noting that Honduras is producing less and that *campesinos* are abandoning the countryside, Juan Antonio Aguirre of the Interamerican Institute of Agricultural Sciences (IICA) said that Honduras faces a "terrifying future" if corrective measures are not taken. He said that the country's current agricultural crisis will become truly catastrophic in the 1990s.[23]

During the 1980s the true dimensions of the agricultural crisis were somewhat hidden and distorted by the large U.S. food-assistance program. Through the PL480 Title I program, Honduras received $15 to $19 million annually in food imports. The program eased the country's balance-of-payments crisis by allowing it to increase its grain imports without having to expend scarce foreign exchange. It also helped ease urban unrest by keeping wheat-flour products available and relatively low-priced.[24]

The food-aid program, while temporarily disguising the severity of the agricultural crisis, has seriously impacted local food production. The influx of relatively cheap foodstuffs has resulted in disincentives for local grain producers and has acted to change consumption patterns. An AID-contracted study found that wheat imports (95 percent of which are covered by the food-aid program) have undermined the market price of corn for farmers, who, as a result, are cutting back on corn production.[25] Because wheat has become relatively cheaper and often more easily available, Hondurans have changed their diet to include more wheat products. For example, today only 65 percent of the population consumes corn as a daily staple, down from about 95 percent 20 years ago.[26] In many cases, families have simply replaced their daily fare of *tortillas*, made from Honduran corn, with bread and pastry made from wheat imported from the United States. According to nutritionist Moisés Sánchez, "We're seeing a subtle process of nutritional acculturation, and unless there is an adequate production of food, the country runs the risk of becoming dependent even for its daily bread."[27]

Part of the country's food-security problem is the the result of having food production relegated to small subsistence farms located on the lowest quality agricultural lands. This has been exacerbated by government policies aimed at stimulating private investment in the production of nontraditional export crops.

AID is a major promoter, if not the prime engineer, of current Honduran agricultural policy, pumping millions of dollars into programs which seek to increase production of nontraditionals for export, in many cases on farmland previously used to grow basic grains. AID has also pressured the government to terminate all programs designed to protect small grain farmers. According to AID's development philosophy, the economics of comparative advantage and the free world market should guide the country's agricultural policies rather than any commitment to national food security. In practice, this means further opening up the country to grain imports from the United States which consume revenues received from agroexports.

The dangers of dependency on the United States as a main source of food imports and main outlet for exports are highlighted during periods of low world market prices for Honduran export crops. Drops in international market prices for coffee, sugar, and bananas, combined with the expansion of nontraditionals, have led many Honduran *campesinos* to conclude that agriculture has become a high-risk venture. For some this has meant cutting back on area planted, while others—an estimated 100,000 a year—have chosen to migrate to the cities in search of more stable opportunities.

Land Reform

Despite the harsh poverty and inequitable distribution of land and wealth in the Honduran countryside, the existence of land-reform programs has been a major stabilizing factor since the early 1960s.[28] Nonetheless in the last few years the modest reform efforts have ground to a halt and the growing problem of landlessness threatens to break the fragile peace in the 1990s.

Under the Liberal government of Ramon Villeda Morales, in 1961 the National Agrarian Institute (INA) was created to organize rural cooperatives, propose colonization projects, and administer land distribution. International pressure to "democratize" production—one of the main thrusts of the Alliance for Progress—coincided with domestic pressures, and in 1962 the country's first Agrarian Reform Law was passed.

Although in reality very little land was distributed—under 4,000 acres—the program did serve to appease some of the *campesinos'* demands. Since most of the land targeted for redistribution belonged to the state, those who pushed the reform expected little opposition from the landed oligarchy. Similarly, the transnational fruit companies actually stood to gain from the process, as it facilitated their goal of transferring some of their production costs and risks onto small farmers. Nonetheless, with a myopia reminiscent of Guatemala a decade earlier, the oligarchy and fruit companies considered Villeda's reforms too radical, and together with conservative sectors in the military, conspired to overthrow his government.

In the wake of the resulting military coup INA's budget was drastically cut and its personnel completely replaced. The ensuing period of repression of *campesino* activism led many groups to resort to the illegal land occupations which became widespread in the early 1970s.

Responding to the growing pressure from the peasantry, the government changed tactics and and adopted a decidedly reformist stance. New, more comprehensive agrarian-reform laws passed in 1972 and 1975 placed ceilings on landholdings and required cattle ranchers to intensify their production. The project aimed to stimulate more productive use of farmland and to address *campesino* demands through the distribution of idle or underexploited properties. But the ceilings were generously high and all lands used for producing export crops, which included the transnationals, were exempted from the law. Between 1972 and 1975, the most dynamic years of the agrarian reform, about 300,000 acres were distributed to some 35,000 families, only one-fourth of the amount demanded by the National Front of United Peasants since 1965 and far short of the goals the government itself had set.

In 1975 conservative military leaders acceded to pressures from the oligarchy and put an end to the reform experiment. Since then, despite promises of the civilian governments of the 1980s, the agrarian-reform process has slowed to a trickle, the victim of a marked lack of political will and cumbersome bureaucratic obstacles, and corruption and inefficiency at INA.

Finding all other avenues closed, the well-organized peasantry has responded with direct action in the form of land occupations. Most occupations take place on idle lands which fall within the bounds of the existing agrarian-reform legislation. Hundreds of small-scale occupations have taken place spontaneously in farming communities throughout the country and there have also been several nationally coordinated actions designed to pressure the government into carrying through with its own agrarian-reform law. The largest such action to date took place in May 1989, when some 400 *campesino* organizations affiliated with the COCOCH umbrella organization staged land invasions on an estimated total of 50,000 acres around the country.[29]

The state has responded ambiguously to *campesino* land invasions. On occasions, it has simply turned a blind eye or invited *campesino* leaders to negotiate settlements of claims through INA. But the most common response has been to send in the army. Many peasants participating in such actions have been jailed, tortured, and killed by the military or by the landowners' private guards. Repressive legislation passed in 1982 defines land invasions as "terrorist acts."

Meanwhile, with genuine land reform on ice in the 1980s, the government has instead pushed a land-titling program. Many *campesino* organizations see this AID-sponsored program as a way of dividing the peasantry. Its major thrust is to provide legal claim to lands which farmers have been working for years, in some cases generations, as a way to facilitate access to credit. The program thus completely fails to address the most pressing problem in the countryside, that of the tens of thousands of *campesino* families with no land at all.

While the mere existence of reform legislation and occasional attempts to rent, grant, or provide title to land have contributed to avoiding the outbreak of widespread rural violence, in reality there are today more landless families in Honduras than before the 1972 law.[30] Since the program's inception over 25 years ago, about 768,000 acres have been distributed to some 70,000 families.[31] In contrast, just ten years of agrarian reform in neighboring Nicaragua gave almost 7 times as much land to 120,000 families.[32]

But numbers do not tell the whole story. While there are some examples of cooperatives receiving good land and generous levels of credit and technical assistance, most *campesinos* affected by the reform have received land which is only marginally suited for agriculture. Likewise, the government's credit policy overwhelmingly favors the large private farms producing export crops. The lack of marketing outlets forces most peasants to sell their excess production to unscrupulous middlemen.[33] As a result of these limitations, INA estimates that as many as one of every four *campesinos* who received land from the agrarian-reform process has since abandoned it.

As in El Salvador and Guatemala, the overriding factor which has impeded efforts at land reform is the absence of political will on the part of the country's rulers. Much of Honduras' best agricultural lands, currently in the hands of big private growers or transnationals, is underutilized or lies idle. With austerity on the horizon and the present emphasis on boosting exports, prospects for land redistribution to the peasantry are bleak. Although pressure from the landless can be expected to mount, it appears unlikely that the new administration of Rafael Callejas—who comes from one of the country's biggest landowning families—will opt for a change of course.

Faced with this panorama of growing hardships and polarization in the countryside, some Hondurans remain confident that a judicious mix of repression, cooptation and limited reform will continue to be effective in containing peasant unrest. Others, such as former Labor Minister Gautama Fonseca, are less optimistic: "We'd be fooling ourselves if we said the future looked bright. Most of the *campesinos* are poor and illiterate. Our schools and universities are appalling, so we're not turning out qualified technicians. As bad as our production levels are now, they will undoubtedly decline even further. Add to that a dominant class which has no interest in solving the problems of the poor and you've got a time bomb. I have no doubt that the future of Honduras will be the same as that of Guatemala, El Salvador, and Nicaragua—that of great social upheaval and civil war."[34]

Industry and Finance

Honduras has the smallest industrial sector in Central America. Little of its industrial output is marketed outside the region except for the textiles and other products assembled by the country's few drawback manufacturing plants. The industrial sector employs about 15 percent of Honduran workers and accounts for a quarter of the country's GDP, while manufactured goods contribute one-fifth of export earnings. Mining, forestry, tourism, and construction are all relatively marginal activities in economic terms.

More than half of all manufacturing enterprises are small, family-owned shops with fewer than ten employees. A full 40 percent of Hondurans employed in manufacturing are classified as artisans, not factory workers. The country's large, modern factories are in the hands of foreign companies or the Honduran business elite. The country's two major banana companies are also among the largest manufacturers. Castle & Cooke produces soap, plastic products, cans, boxes, and cement, while United Brands makes rubber, plastics, margarine, and vegetable oil.

The protected regional markets erected under the provisions of the Central American Common Market (CACM) did stimulate significant growth of Honduran industry in the 1960s, but the boom years did not last long. With the onset of recession in the early 1980s, industry began a decline from which it has still not recovered. Virtually all manufacturing subsectors have stagnated or declined during the 1980s as a result of contracting internal demand, a closing off of regional export markets, tight credit and rising import prices. Structural-adjustment programs that liberalize foreign trade and pull down tariff barriers represent a further threat to local industries that cannot compete with foreign products.

While the local manufacturing sector is stagnating, there has been some growth in export-oriented manufacturing. In 1976 the government opened the doors of the Puerto Cortés Free Zone as part of a policy to attract foreign investment in industry. Enterprises investing in space at the industrial park may import raw materials and semi-finished products without tariffs or duties and freely re-export finished goods, and profits are exempt from taxation. But a variety of constraints have resulted in less than expected growth. By 1987 the Free Zone had attracted only 19 firms, many of which were clothing manufacturers from South Korea, Taiwan, and Hong Kong seeking to transfer to sites like Honduras where they could take advantage of low labor costs and avoid U.S. import quotas.[35]

Honduras remains convinced that such reassembly-for-export ventures hold promise, and accordingly four additional industrial parks are under construction, like the Puerto Cortés park all on the North Coast. The country hopes to attract investment to the parks from 160 firms and generate 30,000 jobs between 1990 and 1995.[36]

Chapter 4

Society and Environment

Popular Organizing

Historically Honduran society has been the least organized in Central America. This lack of social organization paralleled the country's historic lack of political, economic, and even geographical unity. It was not until after World War II that Honduras began to pull together as a national state with a professional army, a central bank, transportation network, and diversified economy. Until 1950 the country's two main cities— Tegucigalpa and San Pedro Sula—were not even connected by a paved road. Before the 1950s there were no private-sector organizations with a national reach, and the few popular organizations that existed were also concentrated in a few geographical pockets.

The "Great Banana Strike" of 1954

It was the banana strike on the North Coast in 1954 that proved to be the watershed for subsequent popular organizing in Honduras. This historic strike was built on a foundation of worker organizing that dates back to the 1920s when the Honduran Labor Federation, associated with the Honduras Communist Party, began to organize banana and mine workers. These early organizers faced constant repression by company and government police. Often forced to operate clandestinely, they made little headway in forming labor unions or bringing other popular sectors into their fight against the dictatorship of Tiburcio Carías Andino (1933-1949) and other unsympathetic government leaders.

The long years of organizing among the banana estates of Standard Fruit and United Fruit were not wasted. This committed labor organizing by leftist unionists in the first half of the 1900s became the base of a hugely successful strike in 1954 against the banana companies. The 1954 strike against United Fruit soon spread throughout the country, eventually shutting down 60 percent of the national economy.

The crisis caught the attention of American Federation of Labor (AFL) president George Meany and the closely associated Interamerican Regional Organization of Workers (ORIT). The U.S. labor hierarchy, working closely with the State Department, was concerned about the leading role of Communist Party organizers in the strike. In the interests of heading off the creation of a strong anti-imperialist workers' movement, Meany urged United Fruit to reach a settlement with the less militant workers and to grant union recognition.[1]

The AFL, CIO, and ORIT pledged funds for an effort to take the initiative away from the more militant strike leaders and to form an anticommunist union movement. AFL representative Serafino Romauldi succeeded in persuading the country's archbishop to circulate a pastoral letter urging workers to join the AFL/ORIT-affiliated unions and calling for the government to enact labor legislation. After the arrest of key strike leaders and their replacement with a more conciliatory Central Strike Committee, United Fruit agreed to negotiate. The strike settlement gave ORIT and its U.S. backers an important inroad into the Honduran labor movement — one that continues today among the country's labor unions and peasant associations.[2] The 1954 strike was, nonetheless, a major victory for Honduran workers. It opened the way for labor and peasant organizing throughout the entire country and established for the first time the tremendous power of the country's popular sectors.

The Social Christian Movement

Before the 1960s the Catholic church had little to do with social issues, confining its social work to charitable programs. (See Religion) But beginning in 1961 the church became a major influence in the development of popular organizing in Honduras. It established new social-service organizations and popular-education programs, while encouraging the formation of peasant leagues.

Running parallel and sometimes closely integrated with the church's various programs in social assistance and development was the Social Christian movement. This new popular movement received financial support from Christian Democratic and Christian Socialist organizations in Europe. It stressed the importance of addressing social-justice issues within the context of capitalism and guided by Christian teachings.[3]

In the 1960s and early 1970s the Social Christian movement gave birth to numerous private organizations, peasant associations, and unions. Among the organizations established with Social Christian inspiration were: Honduran Popular Cultural Action (ACPH, 1961), Social Christian Peasant Association (ACASCH, 1963), Social Christian University

Front (FRESC, 1963), Human Promotion Association (APRHU, 1965), Honduran Development Foundation (FUNHDESA, 1969), Pre-Federation of Consumer Cooperatives, and the Institute of Social-Economic Investigations (IISE, 1973). The Social Christian movement organized politically in 1968 as the Christian Democratic Movement of Honduras (MDCH).

In 1971 the social-promotion organizations of the Catholic church and those of the Social Christian movement came together under a new umbrella organization called CONCORDE (Coordinating Council for Development). CONCORDE was created to coordinate the various programs of its member organizations. Named as the first CONCORDE executive secretary was Rodolfo Sorto Romero, the ex-director of CARITAS, a MDCH supporter, and an adherent of the theology of liberation. The founding organizations of CONCORDE were the following: Catholic Relief Services (CRS), CARITAS, the Catholic church's Social Communication division (which included four radio stations and one weekly newspaper), the church's nine peasant training centers, Federation of Savings and Credit Cooperatives (FACACH), FUNHDESA, and APRHU.

Standing outside but closely associated with many CONCORDE members was the General Workers Central (CGT), the union federation supported by the international and local Social Christian movement. CGT's most prominent member has been the National Campesino Union (UNC), whose leaders were the largely the product of the Catholic church's training and organizing programs.

The close alliance between the Catholic church and MDCH was short lived. A year after CONCORDE was founded, the church hierarchy began pulling its organizations out of the umbrella group. The prelates were concerned that the church's own social-promotion program was becoming too secularized and too closely associated with militant popular organizations. It also felt that the MDCH was using the church for its own political ambitions.

The institutional church's split from CONCORDE marked the beginning of the hierarchy's attempt to distance itself from rural land struggles and other militant expressions of the popular movement for social justice. The church was concerned that by aligning itself too closely with secular political and popular movements it was endangering its own institutional stability and its traditional place in the Honduran power structure.[4]

Peasant Organizing

The first peasant organizations, like the country's first unions, resulted largely from the work of organizers associated with the Honduras Communist Party. One of the first peasant associations was the Central Committee of Peasant Unity, founded in the mid-1950s and later reorganized as the National Federation of Honduran Peasants (FENACH). From the beginning, FENACH was targeted by the security forces. In 1963, after the military coup that overthrew the Villeda government, FENACH's offices were destroyed and its leaders imprisoned.

Along with the military and the church, the AFL-CIO and ORIT were also preoccupied with the FENACH's leftist activism. In 1962 the National Association of Peasants (ANACH) was formed to counteract the influence of FENACH within the peasantry and to assert "democratic" control over the incipient peasant movement. Traditionally ANACH, which is a member of the Confederation of Honduran Workers (CTH), has exerted a conservative influence but in recent years has adopted some of the more confrontational tactics of other peasant groups and has joined in coalitions with leftist union federations. Its long-time president, Julín Méndez, has served as a congressional deputy with the social-democratic Innovation and Unity Party (PINU).

The National Peasant Union (UNC), founded in 1970, has also been a strong influence among the Honduran peasantry. Having strong roots within the Social Christian movement, UNC grew out of the Social Christian Peasant Association (ACASCH) and is a member of the General Workers Federation (CGT). Its major figure has been Marcial Caballero, who in the 1980s has moved steadily toward a position of collaboration with the government, political parties, and the army. Splits between conservative and progressive factions have divided the UNC in recent years, with the Caballero faction maintaining control of association's finances and institutional apparatus. Like the CGT, the UNC has become closely associated with the National Party.[5] It has alienated itself from other forces within the peasant movement by making separate deals with the National Agrarian Institute (INA). In the early 1980s elements within the armed forces suspected the UNC of being a guerrilla front, but a joint corn-production project with the military in Olancho, which got off the ground in 1989, provided further evidence of how far the UNC had moved from its former combative stance.

The most dynamic and progressive peasant federation is the National Union of Rural Workers (CNTC), founded in 1985 mainly from split-offs from ANACH and UNC. This peasant confederation includes: National Union of Peasant Cooperatives (UNACOOPH), National

Authentic Union of Honduran Peasants (UNCAH), Unitary Federation of Peasant Cooperatives (FUNACH), and Front of Independent Honduran Peasants (FRENACHINH). The U.S. embassy charges that CNTC has a Marxist bent because of its working relationship with the leftist FUTH labor federation, but its politics would better be described as progressive social-democratic.[6]

The Federation of Agrarian Reform Cooperative (FECORAH), founded in 1970, is closely linked to the government's National Agrarian Institute and is generally conservative. The Honduran Peasant Organization (OCH) was formed in July 1989 in split from UNC. The Coordinating Committee of Peasant Organizations (COCOCH), which includes CNTC, ANACH, UNC, and FECORAH, is the latest attempt to unify the divided peasant movement.

Recently formed is the Association for Development of the Western Region (ADRO), which brings together 3,500 peasants. ADRO president Eusebio Ramos, summarizing the feelings of most Honduran peasants, said: "For years the government has been coming into our villages and giving us promises. Either there is no action at all, or all the money is wasted on a few cars and on salaries for people who don't do anything."[7] The independence of peasant associations from the government is a major concern in Honduras where the government and the military have had a long history of intervening in and controlling the popular movement with the purpose of neutralizing protests and isolating more militant elements.[8]

There are numerous women peasant organizations including the Honduran Federation of Peasant Women (FEHMUC), the Council for the Integrated Development of Peasant Women (CODIMCA), and the National Association of Peasant Women (ANAMUC), which is an auxiliary of ANACH. (See Women)

Expanding Popular Movement

Before the 1980s the popular movement was largely limited to worker, peasant, and student groups. Over the last ten years, however, the movement has gained broad dimensions with the formation of human rights groups, ethnic and Amerindian organizations, a major research center, women's organizations, and new popular coalitions.

The strength and integrity of popular organizations in Honduras have long been limited by their association with the major political parties, government institutions, the armed forces, and foreign funding organizations. Another weakness of the popular movement in Honduras has been its economism and opportunism—often limiting itself to economic demands and frequently ready to collaborate with the government and armed forces in pursuit of short-term goals.

This tradition of collaboration and compromise has had its rewards. Recognizing the disruptive potential of the popular movement, the political parties and military have occasionally responded to worker and peasant demands. A labor code was adopted, an agrarian-reform program instituted, and price controls and minimum wage laws decreed. Yet for all this history of social compromise, the Honduran population remains among the poorest and most downtrodden in Latin America.

In response to the worsening economic conditions and intensifying repression of the 1980s, the popular movement has gathered new strength and unity. It is still too weak, divided, and unsure of its political direction to present a serious challenge either to the national-security doctrine of the armed forces or the economic policies of the political elite and oligarchy. But there are clear signs that the popular sectors may be able to build on past strengths and develop a national movement capable of mounting such a challenge in the 1990s.

In addition to the peasant organizations already named, Honduras now has several women's organizations (See Women), human rights organizations (See Human Rights), combative student associations (See Students), and a strong labor movement (See Labor). The two small political parties—Christian Democratic Party (PDCH) and the Innovation and Unity Party (PINU)—play an important role in the expanding popular movement. The more leftist Honduran Patriotic Front (FPH) is another political party that is again beginning to organize. (See Politics) In recent years Honduras has also experienced the emergence of community groups which have mounted militant demonstrations demanding better government services and lower prices for basic goods.

Two popular coalitions were formed in the 1980s. The Coordinating Committee of Popular Organizations (CCOP), founded in late 1984, brings together unions, peasant associations, student organizations, and groups of slum dwellers. Among the organizations included in the CCOP coalition are the Union of Electrical Workers (STENEE), the United Revolutionary Front (FRU) at the national university, the United Federation of Honduran Workers (FUTH), and the Visitación Padilla Women's Committee. CCOP has strongly condemned repression of the popular movement and has consistently expressed opposition to U.S. intervention in Central America. Juan Almendres, a former rector of the National University, and Gladys Lanza, STENEE president, are leading figures within CCOP.

The more recently formed popular coalition is the Unified Popular Alliance (APU), formerly known as the Francisco Morazán Patriotic Committee. The APU also represents a variety of popular organizations, including the Texaco refinery union, the Organization of Honduran Peasants (based in the north), League of Patriotic Women, the student-based United Revolutionary Front (FUR), and the Committee of the Ejidos (common municipal land).[9] Like CCOP, APU organizations and leaders have been subject to police and military repression. A third popular coalition is Popular Unity, a San Pedro-based coalition that serves as a coordinated front for ten popular organizations. In general, the popular movement in San Pedro Sula is more dynamic than the one based in Tegucigalpa.

Although the popular sectors have taken some steps to form coalitions, these efforts continue to be undermined by political sectarianism, personality differences, police infiltration, and internecine violence. These and other factors obstruct the kind of unity necessary to confront the escalating repression and deteriorating socioeconomic conditions.

Labor and Unions

Since the landmark strikes of 1954 the Honduran union movement has been seen as the region's largest and strongest.[10] Currently about 15 percent of the total workforce – and some 40 percent of urban workers – belong to unions. Union organizing encompasses three broad sectors of the economy: tens of thousands of Hondurans employed by the state; wage earners in agriculture; and the relatively small industrial workforce.

Honduran unions and peasant organizations have fought hard for their position as influential actors on the national political scene; few governments over the past 30 years have attempted to ride roughshod over their demands, and several have tried to integrate them into broad coalitions. But attempts to divide the movement, sectarian practices, and opportunistic leadership have often diluted its strengths. In addition, despite legal gains won by unions – such as a progressive labor code and minimum wage legislation – enforcement has largely paralleled the government and private sector's ability to pay, and has been limited to the small, modern sector of the economy which employs skilled labor. Particularly with the onset of the economic crisis of the 1980s, there has been widespread noncompliance and the brunt of the burden of structural adjustment of the economy has been shifted to wage-earners who have seen their purchasing power shrink year after year since 1981.

Origins and Rise of Unions

Labor organizing got its start in Honduras after the turn of the century in the U.S. mining and banana enclaves. Harsh economic conditions and the anti-labor policies of the foreign companies — which often called in the Honduran army to help quell worker unrest — created fertile ground for the growth of militant union activity.

After a long period of clandestine and relatively isolated activities, a major turning point came for Honduran trade unions with a 1954 strike which began on the banana plantations (See Popular Organizing). Workers in related areas — such as the railroads, ports, and mines — soon joined in solidarity and the strike eventually encompassed some 50,000 workers. The 1954 strike cast the union movement onto center stage as a force to be reckoned with. The government soon instituted the country's first national labor code, including complete union legalization and recognition of the rights to strike, to organize, and to demand a minimum wage. A revised labor code passed in 1958 provided for paid vacations and severance pay.

But the unprecedented show of worker solidarity in 1954 provoked other responses as well. In an effort to defuse the growing militancy and channel organizing sentiments into more acceptable paths, the American Institute for Free Labor Development (AIFLD) and ORIT began assisting the creation of passive, alternative unions. In the space of a few years, Honduras became the headquarters for this type of U.S.-sponsored union activity in Latin America. By 1960 compliant ORIT-linked unions set up on the banana plantations had acceded to a 50 percent reduction in workforce by both United and Standard Fruit Companies.

In 1964 most of the pro-ORIT federations — including the most powerful of the banana workers' unions and the largest peasant organization, the National Association of Honduran Peasants (ANACH) — came together to form the Honduran Confederation of Workers (CTH). The CTH was the dominant force in legal union activities throughout most of the 1960s and 1970s and, despite recent challenges by newer groups, it remains the largest confederation in Honduras today, claiming 142,000 workers. CTH-affiliated unions can be found in almost all sectors of the economy.

The CTH defines itself as social democratic. Although the confederation has no formal links with any political party, several members from its leadership council have run in national elections as candidates with the PINU. Although there is ample diversity among member unions, the CTH as a whole has worked closely with the government and for the most part has confined its activities to the search for immediate worker benefits.

The second national confederation, the General Confederation of Workers (CGT), was formed in 1970 but was refused legal recognition until 1984. Originally linked to the more conservative sectors of the Christian Democratic Party, conflicts over strategy and patronage have divided both the leadership and the base of the CGT since its founding. Today, the CGT enjoys close ties with the National Party. In fact, several of the confederation's leaders stepped down in order to run for office on the National Party slate in 1989, including one of Callejas' three vice president designates Marco Tulio Cruz. The CGT leaders turned politicians have come out in support of Callejas' strategy of "selling" Honduras to foreign investors, insisting that it is the only way to create new jobs. The CGT base has adopted a more critical stance. The CGT claims to represent 120,000 members, some two-thirds of whom come from the peasant groups of the National Peasant Union (UNC). Internationally, the CGT is affiliated with the Latin American Workers Central (CLAT) and the World Federation of Labor (WCL). In the 1980s CGT unions have received assistance from several Western European Social and Christian Democratic foundations.

The more radical Unitary Federation of Honduran Workers (FUTH) was formed in 1978 and awarded legal status in 1989. The FUTH claims 30,000 workers. Although this makes it by far the smallest of the three national confederations, the FUTH's vocal stance on burning political issues — together with the fact that its membership encompasses strategic areas of the economy such as workers from the Central Bank, the National University, electricity and water companies, and construction — has given the group a high profile.

In some cases together with the more conservative CGT, and increasingly even with the CTH, the FUTH has promoted a broad agenda among labor during the 1980s, including issues such as opposition to the contra and U.S. military presence and respect for human rights. Several FUTH leaders have been assassinated or disappeared, allegedly by the security forces.

The latest addition among the labor confederations is the Independent Federation of Honduran Workers (FITH) founded in 1985. Based in San Pedro Sula, FITH member unions include municipal workers unions and small industrial unions.

Divisions and infighting — in some cases over legitimate political and ideological differences, in others the product of deliberate policies pursued by management and the government — continue to characterize the Honduran union movement. The three major confederations stand worlds apart on many issues. Nonetheless growing hardships brought on by the economic crisis and austerity policies have led to increasing levels of programmatic unity within the movement.

Concretely, during the 1980s, three key issues led to the waging of several major strikes and to an unusual degree of unity within the union movement: 1) calls for a raise in the minimum wage in the face of ever-declining purchasing power; 2) the fight against large-scale layoffs as cutbacks or closures on factories and farms increasingly outpaced the creation of jobs through new investments; and 3) efforts to prevent the penetration of *solidarismo*.

In another expression of the growing tendency towards trade union collaboration around common demands, the country's four major federations – CTH, CGT, FUTH, and FITH – united around a series of issues for the May 1st International Workers Day celebrations in 1989. Common ground was reached on opposition to the presence of contras and U.S. troops in Honduras, to devaluation of the currency and other demands made on the government by the IMF, and on anti-union positions adopted by the private sector and government. Likewise, as the initial outlines of the Callejas administration's economic policy began to emerge, pronouncements from the different confederations indicated a further consolidation of the trend towards unity.

Solidarismo

Both the transnationals and Honduran businessmen have embraced *solidarismo* as an effective way of combating traditional trade unionism and of assuring a more compliant workforce. Well established in Costa Rica, the *solidarismo* movement seeks to replace existing unions with worker-owner financial associations.

Efforts to impose solidarity associations in Honduras have taken place both in industry and on the banana plantations, moving to displace existing unions affiliated with all three of the major federations. But so far, they have achieved limited success. Since the mid-1980s only 12 associations have been established, mostly operating in enterprises like liquor, tobacco and bananas, controlled by transnationals. In mid-1988 the leaders of the CTH, CGT, and FUTH jointly petitioned Congress for a reform of the labor code to effectively bar solidarity associations. In December of that year, *solidarismo* was dealt a severe blow when striking workers from the country's most powerful union, SITRATERCO at the United Brands-owned Tela Railroad Company, won their demands to have management renounce its efforts to establish a parallel workers organization.[11]

Schools and Students

Until the late 1950s education in Honduras was the exclusive privilege of those among the middle and upper classes who could afford to send their children to private schools. The reformist government of Ramón Villeda Morales (1957-1963) introduced the concept of public education and began an ambitious school construction program. According to the Honduran constitution, primary education (ages 7 to 14) is obligatory and free. Despite this constitutional guarantee, education remains a privilege in Honduras because of the lack of schools, the poor quality of public education, and the prohibitive cost of educational materials.

Illiteracy is widespread in Honduras, affecting more than 40 percent of the total population and 84 percent in most rural areas.[12] A third of Hondurans do not have any formal schooling.[13] In many isolated areas of Honduras there are no accessible schools or instruction only extends through the third grade.

Of every ten children entering first grade, seven drop out by the sixth grade. Secondary education offers two levels: *ciclo común* which is vocational education and *ciclo diversificado* which prepares students for higher education or for employment. Only 30 percent of Honduran children who enter first grade enter secondary schools, and of those only 8 percent make it to post-secondary institutions.[14]

Even when educational opportunities do exist, the quality of instruction is poor for the following reasons: inadequate teacher training, low pay for teachers, backward teaching methods, corrupt and unqualified administration, and lack of adequate buildings and teaching materials. The country's teachers union has raised demands for a 400 percent increase in salary. Some teachers are not even being paid regular wages but are part of government food-for-work programs. Memorization is the chief and often the only form of instruction.

The National Autonomous University of Honduras (UNAH) is the central higher educational institution in the country. Founded in 1847, UNAH has some 30,000 students enrolled. University branches in San Pedro Sula and La Ceiba form the University Center of the North (CURLA). There are three private universities: the tiny José Cecilio del Valle University established in Tegucigalpa in 1978, the Central American Technological University (UNITEC) founded in 1987 in Tegucigalpa, and the University of San Pedro Sula (USPS).

The U.S. Agency for International Development (AID) began funding USPS in the 1980s to "provide a political counterweight to the traditionally leftist-dominated National University." Through its grants AID is shaping USPS as a business-oriented university with "curriculum emphasis in the skills areas most needed for improving Honduras' competitiveness in world markets: management, finance, international marketing, business law, and the physical and agricultural sciences." AID is also exploring the possibility of arranging a joint program with a U.S. university which "could also act as a 'brain trust' for Honduran industry through consulting work and research."[15] This support for USPS is consistent with other AID programs that promote the privatization of basic services like education and health.

In an evaluation of AID projects in Honduras, Philip Shepherd of Florida International University called the USPS project "probably one of the worst, most politically charged and interventionist projects contemplated by AID at the present." Shepherd called the project an "attempt to create, subsidize, and develop private university education for elites in Honduras" and observed that "various AID project descriptions ooze with ethnocentric contempt for Latin American public university traditions of open admissions, free public higher education, and student-faculty activism."[16]

Privatization of Education

The new influence of private university education complements the strong place of private schools in primary and secondary education. According to one estimate, the more than 800 private educational institutes in the country served 5 percent of primary school students, 50 percent of secondary students, and 3 percent of university students.[17]

The proliferation of private schools is due in large part to the deficiencies and unavailability of public education. Although the private schools do fill the gap created by lack of government attention to education, the private schools have problems of their own. Private education is often viewed simply as a profit-making venture with little attention to quality or accessibility. Teachers at these schools are often paid below-subsistence wages while the directors and owners rake in large incomes from high student fees. In late 1989 the Azcona administration introduced a measure in the National Congress that would allow the government to regulate the level of teacher salaries and the monthly tuition of students.

The proposed law met with strong resistance from the associations of private schools (FENIEPH) and Catholic schools (FENCEPCH) which denounced it as an infringement on free enterprise and an attempt to make education subject to a totalitarian state. They were supported in their opposition by the Honduran Council of Private Enterprise

(COHEP). Joining in support of the proposal was the COLPROSUMAH teachers' union which argued that all teachers should receive a base salary and that they should be hired according to their qualifications, which is often not the case with private schools. It is unlikely that the Callejas administration, a strong defender of private enterprise, will seek to bring private educational institutions under state control.

Student Organizing

Student organizing at UNAH is highly ideological, extremely divisive, and often violent. Until the early 1980s leftist activists exercised strong influence over the student organizations and university council. The Reformist University Front (FRU) lost its influence after having become dogmatic and sectarian, eventually splitting into a pro-Moscow line (*los gordos*) and a Maoist tendency (*los flacos*). As the influence of FRU declined, the dominant student organization became the Democratic University United Front (FUUD), a rightwing organization with close ties to the new conservative university administration. Appointed as university rector in the early 1980s was Osvaldo Ramos Soto, an associate of General Alvarez and the secretary of the APROH rightwing coalition.[18] (See Military) Ramos Soto, who served as FUUD coordinator until he resigned as UNAH rector in late 1987, was succeeded by Omar Casco, a rightwing ideologue who has been accused by some popular organizations of being linked to death squads.[19] (See Paramilitary Organizations)

Student elections at UNAH have long been vigorously contested events. In the late 1980s they have often degenerated into shootings and rock throwing. Molotov cocktails, tear gas, and grenades have also been exchanged in confrontations among the polarized student factions. Leftist student organizations, FRU and the United Revolutionary Force (FUR), have accused FUUD of electoral fraud and use of armed force to maintain its hold on the university's official student bodies like the Federation of University Students (FEUH). In 1989 FUR's presidential candidate was seriously wounded by gunfire.[20] The leftist students have not, however, been the only victims of political violence at the national university. In mid-1989 a rightwing student leader was assassinated and a bomb destroyed the FUUD headquarters. Revolutionary and progressive student groups have also fought among themselves. Nor has political violence been limited to the national university. Other educational institutions like Francisco Morazán Superior Teachers School have also been torn by conflicts between the rightwing student leadership and leftist challengers.

An important progressive force at the UNAH is the university's
Workers Union (SITRAUNAH). The union has denounced repression
at the university and maintains close ties with the CODEH human rights
organization.

Communications Media

Francisco Morazán, the national hero of Honduras, is said to have
brought the first printing press into the country in 1829 to publish his
newspaper *La Gaceta*. Today the country has four daily newspapers, six
television channels (only one of which is nationwide), and 152 radio stations.

The Electronic Media

Because of the high illiteracy and low income of the population, radio
is the medium with the greatest outreach. There are over one million
radios in the country with some 3.5 million weekly listeners.[21] The first
radio station in the country was established in 1929 by the United Fruit
Company in Tela. The two largest radio networks in the country are
HRN — The Voice of Honduras which is owned by Emisoras Unidas of
the Ferrary-Villeda family and Radio América which is owned by the
leader of the PINU political party and often broadcasts news about
worker and peasant issues. Radio Honduras is the government station.
Both the Catholic church and the evangelical community have radio stations. Unlike the evangelical station, Radio Católica has little religious
programming.

All television stations are privately owned and based either in San
Pedro Sula or Tegucigalpa. Television was introduced in 1959, and about
one-quarter of Hondurans now have access to television sets. Emisoras
Unidas dominates television broadcasting, owning channels 3, 5, and 7 in
Tegucigalpa and channels 4 and 7 in San Pedro Sula. Becoming increas-
ing competitive are the channels of Vica Televisión ("Voz e Imagen de
Centro América") which is owned by the Sikaffy family and other busi-
ness investors in San Pedro Sula.[22]

The Print Media

Tiempo, arguably the country's most influential daily, is owned by
Jaime Rosenthal, a banker and the controversial second vice president
during the Azcona government. Based in San Pedro Sula, *Tiempo* has a
circulation of 32,000 and is the country's most liberal newspaper. Unlike

the other papers, *Tiempo* has often criticized the military and police and regularly publishes liberal opinion articles. Its editor, Manuel Gamero, has on occasion been jailed for his critique of the military and police. Conservatives and military hardliners have called the paper "communist." Even though *Tiempo* does regularly criticize the government and armed forces, its reporting still shows signs of self-censorship.

La Prensa (circulation 42,000) is also based in San Pedro Sula and has close links with the commercial and industrial interests of that city. Its editorial direction is conservative, extremely anticommunist, and pro-United States. Jorge Larach is the president and editor of *La Prensa*.

El Heraldo, based in Tegucigalpa with a circulation of 37,000, is also owned by the Larach family. It too is conservative and often closely reflects the opinions of the military and the National Party.

La Tribuna, based in Tegucigalpa with a circulation of 38,000, is owned by the Flores Facussé family and is linked to the new industrial sector of Tegucigalpa. *La Tribuna* reflects the opinions of the orthodox Liberal Party and is considered moderate and nationalistic in its editorial direction.

The government publishes its decrees and speeches in *La Gaceta*. There is an English-language weekly called *Tegucigalpa This Week*. AVANCE, a businessmen's group funded by the U.S. Agency for International Development (AID), publishes *El Agricultor*, a tabloid that attempts to reach the peasant population. The Honduras Documentation Center (CEDOH), founded in 1980 and directed by Victor Meza, publishes a valuable monthly bulletin of news and analysis called *Boletín Informativo*. Honduras also has several magazines, including the progressive *Presente*; the progressive literary review *Tragaluz*, the centrist business magazine *Cambio*, and the centrist review *Prisma*.

Quality of the News

Repression, self-censorship, dependence on U.S. sources and programming, an environment of corruption and payoffs, poor technical quality, and the control of the media by oligarchic interests are all factors explaining the dismal state of news reporting in Honduras. The Honduran media practices self-censorship described this way by Honduran poet Roberto Sosa: "In Honduras open censorship does not exist, but rather a more subtle form of censorship: self-censorship. Honduran reporters have not actually disappeared. But they have disappeared as thinking and inquisitive journalists, and this is worse. They are like zombies."[23]

Media owners and journalists are careful not cross an invisible line of what can and cannot be reported, especially about the contras and the military. *Tiempo* is the media outlet that has been most daring in walking the fine line between what is permissible and not permissible. One ex-columnist for *Tiempo* described this invisible line: "Every reporter knows the limit of the truth of the owners and has to write within those limits. It is a very sophisticated system and the hardest part is to see it. It is more difficult than official censorship, although the results are the same."[24] *Tiempo's* Gamero further explained that "Honduras isn't like Guatemala or El Salvador where the repression is of a different magnitude. In our country, the methods of repression are tolerable, relatively speaking. The problem that exists is that there is much manipulation of the press by the government and the private sector. Neither of those sectors believes that the public has the right to be informed."[25]

When journalists do cross the line they are subject to arrest, harassment, blacklisting, violence, and deportation in the case of foreign reporters. After Rodrigo Wong Arevalo, the director of Radio América, aired a series of editorials opposing the contras in 1986, a car bomb exploded outside his house. Other Honduran reporters have been arrested and threatened by military intelligence. But the most common form of punishment is firing and blacklisting.[26] According to the Council on Hemispheric Affairs, "Virtually every news organization as well as the Colegio de Periodistas (association of reporters), has yielded to government pressure to adhere to an official blacklist of journalists, preventing dissident members of the press from practicing their craft."[27] Foreign journalists, particularly those inquiring too deeply about the relationship between the contras and Honduran military, have been deported or refused permission to enter the country.

The military has made it increasingly clear that it will not tolerate criticism from the media. In early 1989, for example, the attorney general, acting on the request of the military, took Manuel Gamero to court for having "defamed" the military. There are also signs that official censorship is increasing. Lt. Col. Mario Leonel Fonseca, director of the Honduran Telecommunications Company (HONDUTEL) threatened sanctions, including revocation of licenses, if the electronic media transmits "messages coming from subversive persons or groups that attack the security and integrity of the state."[28]

Low pay for journalists contributes to a corrupt system in which reporters regularly receive presents and bribes from the government, businesses, and other institutions seeking favorable reporting. Beginning reporters receive only $250 monthly and senior reporters may get as much as $500 a month. Gratuities and payoffs from the government are quite common. This does not necessarily mean that reporters will not occasionally be critical of the government but that there is little follow-up or investigative reporting.[29]

The pervasive U.S. influence in the Honduran media is a product of both heavy reliance on U.S. news services and television programming and the work of the United States Information Service (USIS). Working out of the U.S. embassy, USIS has a daily distribution program of wireless file material and radio and television programming. Included among its information services are five weekly half-hour programs for 23 radio stations.[30]

The State of Health

The country's deadening poverty is reflected in its deteriorating state of health. According to the Pan American Health Organization, health conditions in Honduras are among the worst in the hemisphere, and a recent study by the United Nations Fund for Children (UNICEF) revealed that malnutrition among Honduran children has worsened in the last two decades.[31] It is estimated that at least 12,000 Honduran children die each year—about 36 daily—from preventable illnesses. The 1989 UNICEF study determined that 25 percent of Honduran families suffer from protein deficiency, 70 percent have inadequate iron intake and 62 percent show calorie deficiency.[32]

Widespread malnutrition and the lack of access to potable water and sanitation facilities are the main factors in the country's low life expectancy (62 years) and high infant mortality (66 per 1,000 live births according to official estimates and 157 per thousand in rural areas according a January 1989 report by the country's teaching hospital).[33] Only one-third of Hondurans have easy access to potable water and 50 percent do not have even the most rudimentary system for human waste disposal.[34]

So widespread is malnutrition that the main public hospital in Tegucigalpa only accepts cases of third-degree or severe malnutrition. In the malnutrition ward at that hospital, ten to 15 children die each month. "And you have to realize," said Judith Castigo, head of malnutrition ward, "that the most desperate children never make it to the hospital. Those are the ones whose families don't have the bus fare to get to the capital, or the 50 cents for the doctor's visit. They die quietly in their homes."[35]

In several areas of the country, severe malnutrition affects a quarter of the children entering first grade.[36] In rural areas 77 percent of the population cannot afford food which would provide them with minimal nutritional requirements.[37] Malnutrition, which had lessened in the 1960s and 1970s, worsened in the 1980s. Dr. Fidel Barahona, a Ministry of Public Health official, warned in 1988 that because of increasing malnutrition coming generations of Hondurans would be mentally and physically less developed.[38]

Infectious and parasitic diseases are the leading causes of death. According to the Ministry of Health, gastritis, enteritis, and tuberculosis are the country's main health problems. Health care is out of the financial and geographic reach for most Hondurans. In the most isolated rural areas there are no doctors or nurses. Although government health clinics do exist, they are often little more than empty buildings without medicines or medical equipment. About 40 percent of the population, however, has no access even to the most rudimentary public health services.[39] According to one report, only 5 percent of Honduran women have had Pap smears — and of these 90 percent registered some abnormality.[40]

Alcoholism and drug addiction are major health concerns in Honduras. At least 6,000 Hondurans belong to a narrow category of alcoholics called *pachangueros* who drink a dangerous mixture of water and straight alcohol. Thousands of Honduran youth are glue addicts. According to a government mental health doctor, as many as 150 children die each year from inhaling a widely advertised brand of glue called Resistol.

The first known Honduran victim of AIDS died in May 1985, and by the end of the decade 248 cases of the disease were registered. Health authorities, however, estimate that over 7,000 Hondurans carry the infection and that this number will likely rise to 25,000 by 1991. Forty-five percent of the AIDS cases reported thus far have been heterosexuals. Many Hondurans place the blame on the spread of AIDS on the influx of U.S. servicemen. Although prostitution has boomed around the Soto Cano air base (formerly Palmerola) where the U.S. troops are stationed, the country's poor health conditions and lack of education are probably the main reasons for the rapid spread of the fatal infection. Dr. José Enrique Zelaya, chairperson of the National AIDS Commission, said, "Problems related to poverty and lack of health maintenance mean AIDS is hitting a population that is already weak."[41]

Another factor in the spread of AIDS may be the repeated use of disposable needles. Rather than going to a doctor, poor Hondurans often pay 50 cents to those advertising "Injections Applied." Nurses and hospital aides are known to collect disposable syringes and needles from hospital trash baskets to take home to use in their moonlighting businesses.[42]

Honduras suffers at the same time from both a proliferation and a shortage of medicines. Estimates by the Ministry of Public Health show that over 17,000 medicines are available in the country. But a random sampling by a research team at the national university found that only 61 percent of the medicines encountered at pharmacies were of any value. The report concluded that the Honduran market was flooded with ineffective and unapproved products that were dumped by U.S. and European producers. According to the World Health Organization, 300 drugs are sufficient to meet most health problems. The flood of medicines means that pharmacists are often prescribing drugs that are untested and may be harmful.[43]

A more pressing problem, however, is the lack of medicines in public health facilities. The ever worsening foreign-exchange crisis and new austerity measures have meant that there is less money available to import needed drugs. Even when hospitals do have medical supplies, they quickly disappear due to the widespread practice of stealing drugs from government health care facilities to sell to private drugstores.[44]

An even larger problem is the widespread lack of access to health services and the limited reach of social security. The Ministry of Health has concluded that only 40-50 percent of the population has access to health services and that only 11 percent of the population is protected by the Honduran Institute of Social Security — despite constitutional guarantees of health care and social security services.[45]

Religion

The Roman Catholic Church is the oldest and most powerful religious institution in Honduras. The arrival in 1521 of Franciscan missionaries with the Spanish conquistadores gave the church its early foothold.[46] Although the Catholic church has enjoyed more than four and a half centuries in Honduras, it has never developed into a strong, indigenous institution. Instead, it is one of the most dependent churches in Latin America. A symptom of this external dependence is the large number of expatriate clerics. Of the some 292 priests working in Honduras, only about 70 are natives.[47]

The church faced the first major challenge to its institutional power from the country's new political forces in 1821 — the year the region won independence from Spain.[48] Tense relations between church and state persisted until 1838. A reapproachment that year eased tensions between the church and the political elite. In the 1880s the church once again came under attack. The Liberal Party, which was gaining power throughout Central America, set out to dismantle the the feudal-like power of the Catholic church by stripping away its traditional economic and social privileges and establishing the separation of church and state. While substantially weakened, the Catholic church nonetheless remained the semi-official religion of Honduras.

For the Catholic church, the last three decades have been a time of rapid change and constant challenge. In the late 1950s the Catholic hierarchy, encouraged by the Vatican, began a concerted effort to consolidate and strengthen the institutional church. In 1959 the church hierarchy called for an ambitious evangelization campaign to make practicing Catholics out of the large number of Hondurans who were only culturally tied to the Catholic faith.

The call went out from the Vatican to churches throughout the world to send missionaries and financial assistance to Honduras. Priests, brothers, and nuns from the United States, Spain, Canada, and France arrived in Honduras to carry out this mission of church building and evangelization. By the late 1960s the number of dioceses had tripled, with most of them presided over by foreign-born bishops. The new missionaries confronted a nation of deeply religious people, but for most Hondurans, superstition and magic were as least as important as church dogma.

Before the call to evangelize, the social-assistance programs of the Catholic church were disjointed and not linked to any broad vision of social change. Local parishes did sponsor various charitable programs, but there was no institutional commitment to social assistance and community-welfare programs. Catholic Social Action handled individual charity cases but did little to address the structural causes of poverty and hunger.

As the church reached out to rural areas, it found a sea of illiteracy, poverty, and disease. As part of its evangelism, the church tackled these tough socioeconomic problems with literacy and social-service programs. To a large extent, the church's interest in improving *campesino* literacy was a direct outgrowth of its attempt to teach catechism. Rural illiteracy was seen as a main obstacle to bringing church doctrine to the rural poor.

Social Welfare and Anticommunism

The rising interest of the Catholic church in social-assistance programs coincided with the installation in Tegucigalpa of the reformist government of President Ramón Villeda Morales (1957-1963). Although humanitarian concerns certainly played a large part of this new church and government interest in social welfare, anticommunism was the main motivating factor. New economic growth and unprecedented popular organizing in the 1950s and early 1960s indicated that Honduran society was quickly changing, and those sitting in the traditional seats of power wanted to be sure not to lose control of the social situation. Both the church and the government saw social reforms and community-development programs as doses of preventive medicine against the disease of communism.

The progressive government of Jacobo Arbenz in Guatemala and the 1954 strike against United Fruit sparked fears of the possible rise of a leftist-inspired revolution in Honduras. Worries among the church hierarchy about the advance of communism in Central America were heightened by the triumph of Castro's guerrilla forces in Cuba in 1959. Encouraged by the Vatican, the bishops resolved to combat the perceived communist threat and the growing secularization of society. Programs were established to bring workers and peasants back into a revitalized church.

In the 1960s the Catholic church and the incipient Social Christian movement began reaching out to the poor with messages of liberal reform, social betterment, and anticommunism. In 1961 the church began to play a prominent role in the promotion of *campesino* leagues, community-development cooperatives, and other nongovernmental groups. The church hierarchy established such organizations as CARITAS, the Popular Cultural Association of Honduras (ACPH), and the Radio Católica.

Foreign missionaries had enabled the hierarchy to establish new dioceses and parishes, but the need for indigenous clergy persisted. To fill this gap, the church turned to lay workers; many new lay societies like the Legion of Mary and Christian Family Movement were established in the 1960s. A lay catechist movement called the Celebrants of the Word was formed to carry the dogma of the Catholic church to communities seldom visited by clergy.

Although the church hierarchy did become acutely concerned about socioeconomic issues, the prelates always tried to keep the social programs closely linked to religious ones. Institutional stability and growth remained major concerns.

Three Trends:
The Institutional, Developmentalist, and Prophetic Church

The Catholic church is not a monolithic institution. Within the church there are numerous ideological tendencies and geographical divisions. Gustavo Blanco and Jaime Valverde in their book *Honduras: Iglesia y Cambio Social* describe three major tendencies which have evolved within the Catholic church since the late 1950s. These are: the hierarchical church, the developmentalist church, and the prophetic or socially committed church. While each tendency or sector is distinct, none is exclusive.[49] During the last 30 years, each of the three tendencies has gone through periods of dominance and decline.

The hierarchical or institutional church aims to consolidate itself as a strong institution tied to the international church based in Rome. During the 1960s and early 1970s the developmentalist and prophetic tendencies or sectors within the church became more dominant.

To a large degree the developmentalist sector had the same political and economic vision as President Kennedy's Alliance for Progress and the reformist factions within the Honduran military. Within the church, the developmentalist lay workers and clergy not only tended to the spiritual needs of their congregations but also assisted them materially by promoting self-help organizations like cooperatives and housewives' clubs.

Although poor Hondurans were the focus of church-related development programs, poverty in Honduras was thought to be more a problem of lack of education and opportunity than the result of rigid class divisions and unjust social structures. To improve the underdeveloped state of rural communities, the developmentalists advocated such nonconfrontational and legal measures as the formation of savings cooperatives, better education, technical assistance, improved government social services, enforcement of the agrarian-reform laws, and frontier settlement programs for the landless. The salient characteristics of this developmentalism were foreign aid, community organizing, and adherence to Christian principles.

Not all developmentalists, however, were satisfied with this reformist approach to social problems. Within the church's developmentalist sector, many *campesino* leaders and clergy adopted a more radical focus. They saw the limits of developmentalism, and felt that more profound changes were needed to produce true economic and social development in Honduras. They saw the country's problems in terms of institutionalized class rule by the wealthy, and enthusiastically adopted the findings of the Medellín Bishops Conference in 1968 that called for the church's "option for the poor." In doing so, this part of the church — known in Honduras and elsewhere in Central America as the prophetic church — became closely committed to the demands of *campesino* and workers organizations. The prophetic church was also characterized by its strong denunciations of military repression and economic exploitation of the poor. The prophetic tendency (which was most strong in the 1967-1975 period) was closely identified with the theology of liberation and spurred the growth of the *iglesia popular* (popular church), which found its strength in Christian base communities and such activist clergy as Father Guadalupe Carney.

The "Shock of Olancho"

The contradictions among the three different tendencies of the church — hierarchical, developmentalist, and prophetic — were most fully played out in the department of Olancho. Presided over by a North American bishop, the Olancho diocese was the area where the church's commitment to the "option for the poor" was most complete. It was in Olancho, too, where the private-sector elite mounted its strongest opposition to the growing popular movement.

The 1972 killing by the military of six *campesinos* participating in a UNC land takeover signaled the beginning of the repression against the popular movement and the popular church. Three years later, in May 1975, the large landowners and their vigilantes struck out with unprecedented brutality at the local church and *campesino* movement, leaving ten *campesinos*, two female students, and two priests dead. While the church hierarchy did denounce the repression in Olancho, it reduced its own commitment to social-justice issues after 1975.

For the military government and FENAGH (Federation of Honduran Farmers and Ranchers), the "shock of Olancho" had its desired effect. The 1975 massacre was a severe blow to the budding popular church and to the growing popular organizations in Olancho and other parts of the country. The attacks in Olancho were not isolated incidents but part of a mounting repression against the popular church. Foreign priests were expelled, others were arrested, and Catholic radio stations and *campesino* centers were shut down.

The "shock of Olancho" not only undermined the prophetic or socially committed sector of the church but also debilitated the developmentalist faction by making it fearful of the political consequences of even the most nonconfrontational type of social action. After 1975 the church hierarchy pulled far back from its former commitment to such social-justice issues as land reform. It also dramatically cut its commitment to lay organizations affiliated with the institutional church, like the Celebrants of the Word. At the same time that it was backing away from socially active lay groups, the hierarchy was putting renewed emphasis on spiritualist lay organizations like the Charismatic Renewal Movement and the Movement of the New Catacombs. To a large degree, these steps backwards were defensive measures taken to protect the institution in the face of growing persecution. But the church hierarchy also used the incidents in

Olancho as a way to cut off the popular church and its more radical vision of social change.

After the Olancho massacre the institutional church emphasized its moderating role in Honduran society and became more cautious about endorsing the causes of popular organizations. It was eager once again to establish cordial relations with the state in the interests of its own stability and standing within society. The years 1975 to 1981 saw the fading of the prophetic tendency among the church leaders and the suppression of the popular church. Those were also years when social reforms were paralyzed by the military governments. It was a time, too, when the government was more concerned about promoting economic growth and aiding the private sector than about dealing with pressing social issues.

The church also backed away from the aggressive developmentalism that had characterized some of its more prominent social programs. Gone was the emphasis on popular community organization and the call for structural changes in Honduran society. Developmentalism remains a part of the church in the 1980s, but its community-development programs often closely resemble the small-business and productive-enterprise programs that AID and other international donors are currently promoting. After Olancho, the institutional church took several steps backwards to the safe and paternalistic handout programs sponsored by CARITAS and the Christian Family Movement.

A Voice for Social Justice

As social circumstances worsen in Honduras, the church is once again becoming outspoken in its criticisms of the government. And once again there are signs that the prophetic or socially committed church is becoming a stronger force within the Catholic church.

Although the church hierarchy has generally tried to take a conciliatory role, it has been driven to more critical positions in the 1980s. An early break with the Suazo government came with the foundation of APROH (Honduran Association for Progress), an organization that tried to create a new rightwing ideological front in Honduras to support U.S. foreign economic and military policy. APROH was headed by military strongman General Alvarez Martínez and financed by CAUSA, a political arm of Reverend Sun Myung Moon's Unification church. The government's acceptance of this new private organization and the role of the Unification church greatly angered the bishops.

Another factor that pushed the church to assume a more critical posture was the arrival of refugees from Guatemala and El Salvador. The diocese of Santa Rosa de Copán denounced the Honduran military's repression of this refugee population. The local bishop assumed part of the responsibility of caring for the Salvadoran refugees, with CARITAS providing the refugees with food and other services. The Refugee Committee of the diocese has played an important role in drawing national and international attention to these refugees. The killing of two CARITAS workers by the Honduran security forces induced the national church hierarchy to condemn the repressive conditions in the country.

The worsening economic conditions in the country, the new militarism fueled by the United States, and the failure of the Suazo and Azcona governments to address the needs of the nation's poor have been other factors that caused the institutional church to become more outspoken about social issues in the 1980s. The creation of groups within the church like the Christian Movement for Justice and the continuing experience of the clergy in rural areas also pushed the church to assume a more committed social role in Honduran society.

Gradually, during the 1980s, the bishops increased their denunciations of the government and military — but always as diplomatically as possible. At the same time, though, the bishops denounced the purported links between the popular church and Marxists, which tended to fortify the military's own campaign against leftist dissidents. Although critical of the growing repression in Honduran society, the institutional church was careful always to align itself on the side of anticommunism.

Foreign clergy and financing, both from the United States and Europe, have been essential in the rise of the developmentalist and socially committed church in Honduras. The Jesuit priests in Yoro and Colón, for example, have played an important role in popular education efforts. Because they operate within their own vicariate, these foreign clergy (from Spain and the United States) have had some measure of autonomy from the generally more conservative Honduran hierarchy. Foreign clergy in Honduras have found themselves subject to deportation by the military. Progressive and popular priests, both foreign and native, have been increasingly targeted for transfers outside the country or to other more conservative or less politically volatile areas.

The rise of evangelicalism presents a major threat to the stability and growth of the Catholic church. To a certain extent, its renewed support for lay organizations with a spiritual focus is part of its effort to counteract the growing appeal of the evangelical churches. The Catholic charismatics and other Catholic spiritualist groups place a new emphasis on the personal relationship of man to God and on the key role of the Holy Spirit. This stress on individualistic faith and salvation is very similar to that of the evangelical churches.

Occasionally, the bishops do excoriate the *evangélicos* (Protestants) for their simplistic approach to religious faith and for their reactionary politics. But in doing so they often lump all evangelicals together — both mainline and pentecostal — thereby exhibiting their superficial understanding of the evangelical community. The failure of the institutional church to address its own weaknesses also contributes to its apparent inability to adequately respond to challenges presented by the evangelical movement in Honduras.

Protestant Churches and the New Evangelicals

In the 1980s evangelical churches and organizations emerged not only as a major religious sector but also as the sponsors of many social-service programs. Evangelical groups, most of which receive U.S. supplies and financing, have also exerted a significant conservative political influence on Honduras.

Among the first evangelical missionaries in the country were Anglican missionaries of the Society of the Gospel in Foreign Parts who began preaching on the North Coast in the 1870s. During the 19th century, Protestant missionary efforts focused on the English-speaking inhabitants of the North Coast, La Mosquitia, and Bay Islands. The British influence in the Atlantic coast facilitated the development of Protestant churches in this region. Another factor was the increasing banana trade with the United States around the turn of the century.

Eventually the traditional Protestant churches extended their mission to the country's interior but they still maintain their strongest bases on the Atlantic side of Honduras. Faith missions from the United States like the Central American Mission helped spread evangelical beliefs of a fundamentalist character throughout Honduras. On a national level, it was not until the 1950s and the 1960s that the evangelical church community began to gain a foothold in this Catholic country.

Hurricane Fifi in 1974 brought in a new wave of evangelical missionaries, mostly from the United States. Until then, the evangelical community consisted largely of traditional Protestant denominations like the Baptists, the Adventists, and fundamentalist mission churches. Pentecostal churches like the Assemblies of God and Church of God increased their membership in the 1970s, and the country began seeing an influx of neopentecostal missionaries, churches, and organizations. Since 1980 pentecostals have set the direction and pace of the evangelical movement. Jimmy Swaggart and Pat Robertson — both of whom have visited Honduras several times — have contributed greatly to evangelical growth through their teleministries.

Between 1978 and 1985 the number of evangelicals in Honduras doubled, and today approximately 12 percent of Hondurans profess to be evangelicals.[50] Only a small number of these belong to mainline liturgical Protestant denominations like the Lutheran church. Most belong to fundamentalist evangelical churches like the Church of God and the Assemblies of God or are members of evangelical pentecostal churches. The balance of this non-Catholic Christian group belong to other churches like the Adventists and the Quakers.

Today the largest evangelical churches in the country are the Assemblies of God, the Southern Baptists, and the Central American Mission. Most evangelical churches in Honduras are closely linked to U.S. denominations and groups, although churches based in Guatemala and El Salvador are also quickly gaining influence.

Free Food and Bibles

Most evangelical churches have social-assistance programs in conjunction with their religious ministries. The most common programs involve education, medical care, and food distribution. These programs are part of what many evangelicals call integral evangelism, meaning the combination of material assistance and spiritual guidance. Humanitarian assistance by the evangelicals usually comes hand-in-hand with Bibles. This assistance — medicine, used clothes, food, toys, and vitamins — comes from a wide variety of evangelical relief organizations including the Larry Jones' Ministries, MAP International, World Concern, World Opportunities International, Friends of the Americas, and Pat Robertson's Operation Blessing. The evangelical humanitarian aid is generally shipped to Honduras on banana boats (courtesy of Standard Fruit and United Brands) or on U.S. military planes (according to the provisions of the Denton Amendment which allows humanitarian assistance to be shipped on military aircraft on a space-available basis).

World Vision plays a key role in fomenting the growth of evangelical churches and pushing for the integration of social work and evangelizing. World Vision recognizes that there is a close link between evangelical growth and the ability of evangelical organizations to respond in some fashion to the weighty socioeconomic realities of Honduras. In a recent analysis of Honduras and the evangelical presence there, World Vision noted that not only was Honduras undeveloped but it remained poor because of the self-interested behavior of large land owners, business elite, and political bureaucrats.[51] World Vision encourages evangelical churches to become more politically and socially active, noting the resistance of many evangelicals to involve themselves in secular affairs. This call by World Vision for more social and political involvement on the part of evangelicals is part of a regional trend of evangelicals. Rather than isolating themselves from political issues, many evangelicals are doing such things as setting up programs for displaced persons and even forming political parties. The sudden emergence in Guatemala of an evangelical chief of state in 1982 has fueled this trend.

There seems to be little real interest in addressing structural economic problems in the society. The common belief among most evangelicals is that the serious social and economic problems in Honduras are the work of Satan. During his Honduras crusade, Jimmy Swaggart blamed that "shadowy entity" for guerrilla war and poverty in Central America. "Sin is the cause of your problems," he told the listening multitude, "Sin is the cause of your pain." Instead of attacking the social causes of Honduran poverty and injustice, evangelical churches try to allay the symptoms with handout programs while preaching their message of personal salvation.

Most churches have their own assistance programs, although many also rely on teams of evangelical health workers and other religious volunteers to carry out their charitable works. Politically sensitive areas like La Mosquitia are saturated by such volunteer teams, most of whom have few language skills or experience in third world countries. Evangelical teams from the United States also build churches, lead crusades, and direct seminars throughout Honduras.

The pentecostal and neopentecostal groups, most of which are new to Honduras, have often been more aggressive politically than the older evangelical organizations. Indeed, many of them came to Honduras explicitly to fight communism. They chose Honduras for their mission because of the contra war and because they regard the country as a frontline against communism. Allen Dansforth, the U.S. director of World Gospel Outreach, regards social assistance as a weapon against the spread of world communism. Dansforth believes that communists win their base of popular support by providing people with their basic needs and medical care. The evangelical minister believes that by operating social-assistance programs evangelicals "can be a powerful tool to head communism off at the pass, in the name of Jesus Christ."

There is, however, a sector of progressive evangelical organizations that are concerned about social-justice issues and support ecumenism. The Christian Development Commission (CCD), for example, has a reputation for effective, community-based development work. It is also true that while the hierarchy of most evangelical churches is very conservative, evangelical pastors on the local level are more concerned about social-justice issues.

Nongovernmental Organizations

Largely because of the country's important place in U.S. foreign policy in the 1980s, there was a rapid rise in nongovernmental organizations (NGOs) involved in development, refugee relief, business promotion, and social-service operations. Since 1980 the number of NGOs in Honduras has tripled, and most of this increase was in U.S. private and church organizations funded by the U.S. government.[52] Nowhere in Central America was the boom of NGOs linked to the United States so pronounced as in Honduras during the 1980s.

This upsurge in private groups is most noticeable in Tegucigalpa. Green-and-black *Misión Internacional* license plates abound, expatriates frequent a new strip of high-priced clubs and restaurants along Morazán Boulevard, and English-speaking evangelicals are setting up missions in poor and rich neighborhoods alike.

Until 1975 most nongovernmental organizations were linked to the Catholic church or the Social Christian movement. NGOs provided education and training for organized community groups and mass organizations. The few but highly influential organizations shared, for the most part, a common understanding that poor Hondurans suffered from structural injustices in society whose solution was not charity but community organizing.

In the 1960s and early 1970s several NGOs financed by the U.S. Agency for International Development (AID) also began operating in Honduras. These organizations were mostly involved in providing technical assistance, channeling credit, distributing food, or in the case of the American Institute for Free Labor Development (AIFLD) trying to establish a strong conservative pro-U.S. labor sector. Starting in 1962, AIFLD worked through the National Association of Honduran Peasants (ANACH) and the Confederation of Honduran Workers (CTH). Later, AID funds were also channeled to the Federation of Honduran Agrarian Reform Cooperatives (FECORAH). More recently, AID has also channeled funds to the National Campesino Union (UNC), historically one of the more militant of rural organizations.

AID-Funded Boom

The meteoric rise in the number of NGOs operating in Honduras in the last decade is almost totally attributable to AID. In fact, it is now difficult to find NGOs that do not receive AID funds. Dozens of Honduran NGOs have been created with this AID funding, while many U.S.-based NGOs have also opened offices in Honduras. Increased AID support for private voluntary organizations in the 1980s was in keeping with the agency's stated commitment to the privatization of development work.

AID says it supports NGOs as a way to promote pluralism in Honduran society and also because private organizations are more efficient than government agencies. One common concern in Honduras is that it is AID itself which is defining the boundaries of this pluralism. Most AID development funds go to groups that focus on entrepreneurship, export production, or paternalistic community development. Excluded from AID's funding programs are grassroots peasant associations, militant trade unions, progressive development organizations, and human rights groups. In fact, many of these popular organizations would reject AID support even if offered because of their sharp disagreements with the political and economic objectives of AID programs. These organizations receive most of their funding from Europe.

AID does direct some money to rural cooperatives, but the money is mostly used for programs designed to increase export-oriented production and to improve administrative capabilities. In one case, AID encouraged a group of small farmers associated with ANACH to grow chili peppers for export. Promised by AID that markets were available, the small growers worked on chili production for two years but upon attempting to export the chilies these Tela-area farmers found that there were no buyers.

Since 1980 AID has been responsible for the creation of at least ten organizations to promote the interests of the private business sector, particularly those entrepreneurs and investors involved in export production. AID funds also go to established business chambers like the Honduran-American Chamber of Commerce. (See U.S. Economic Aid)

Although most of AID's support for private organizations flows to business organizations and chambers of commerce, AID has also directed funds to an array of service and development groups. AID funding has resulted in the rapid expansion of a small umbrella organization for Honduran NGOs called FOPRIDEH (Federation of Private Development Organizations of Honduras). Most of the AID funds to FOPRIDEH are given to projects that assist small and micro-entrepreneurs. Although Honduran NGOs attempt to maintain some degree of independence, AID's control over FOPRIDEH's finances keeps these NGOs dependent on the U.S. government and aligned with AID's development philosophy.

In addition to the dozens of NGOs that AID funds within the country, the agency also contracts with U.S. organizations like Winrock International and the National Rural Electric Cooperative Association for technical assistance to the Honduran government and other NGOs.

It is difficult to escape the web of financing created by AID. Known as the bountiful *"Señora Aida"* by some NGOs, the agency channels money to most government agencies, the military (through civic-action programs and COPEN's disaster-assistance program), and almost all NGOs. In many cases, government agencies and NGOs do not even know they are using AID money because it comes in the form of *lempiras* which are channeled through the government's central bank. "Everywhere you go you are offered funds which turn out to be Economic Support Funds local currency," observed one NGO director.

Independence vis-a-vis AID is also a concern among a few NGOs. A director of one of the few NGOs that does not accept AID funds put it this way: "Our country is very weak now. We are being manipulated by the United States, and find ourselves just waiting for gifts from the outside." Another NGO representative asserted that the paternalistic and handout nature of AID assistance is not working. "Each day the poverty and underdevelopment are getting worse. The aid is not even keeping up with the growth in poverty and unemployment. The problem is that AID is not interested in funding groups that want to change the system in Honduras; they just want to hand out pills to deaden the pain."

Significantly, it is generally only those NGOs that do not receive AID money that have maintained ties and work closely with the more progressive and independent peasant, worker, and community organizations. These NGOs rely mostly on European funding, and they stress that development work must be done in association with self-organized poor people's organizations.

The direction of development projects sponsored by NGOs in the 1980s is closely related to the question of independence from the government and AID. Only a small number of NGOs in Honduras still espouse the development priorities that were prominent in the 1960s and 1970s. Instead of pressing for peasant leadership training, cooperative formation, and integral popular education, most NGOs now active in Honduras tend to stress such values as profitability, competitiveness, individual enterprise, and marketability.

Women and Feminism

In a region where women are generally consigned to inferior status in society, Honduran women are among the most abused and exploited.

Statistics give one indication of the severity of discrimination against women. Approximately 40 percent of women have no schooling. Only 44 percent of children in primary school are female.[53] Of high school and university graduates, only 25 percent are women. Only 25 percent of the paid workforce are women—yet almost half of all children are born to single mothers who head households.[54] Only one of the 134 deputies in the National Congress is a woman.[55]

Then there is another reality not adequately portrayed by statistics. In a society pervaded by base *machismo*, women are often regarded as little more than sexual prey and cheap labor. The daily newspapers feature pin-ups to sell papers, and the political parties show semi-nude women dancing to sell their candidates. Sexual abuse and rape of young girls by male family members and neighbors is common. Indeed in many poor urban *barrios* few girls make it beyond their early teens without becoming sexual victims.

Activist Elvia Alvarado described life for rural Honduran women: "We women work even harder than the men. We get up before they do to grind the corn and make tortillas and coffee for their breakfast. Then we work all day—taking care of the kids, washing clothes, ironing, mending our husbands' old rags, cleaning the house. We hike to the mountains looking for wood for cutting. We walk to the stream of the well to get water. We make lunch and bring it to the men in the field. And we often grab a hoe and help in the fields. We never sit still one minute."[56]

Irresponsible paternity is a common problem in Honduran society, one particularly widespread in rural areas. A study by the Overseas Education Fund found that 41 percent of the homes in 29 Tegucigalpa neighborhoods were headed by women.[57] In rural Honduras, few women and men marry because of expense and the male-dominated culture. Peasant men commonly leave their wives and children to start new families elsewhere and only rarely feel responsible for the sustenance of all their offspring.

Fertility is the third highest in Latin America, and at least half of Honduran children are born out of wedlock.[58] Contraceptive use is low—about one-third of the population—and abortion is illegal (as it is throughout Latin America with the exception of Cuba). Illegal abortions are available, but many women often resort to self-inflicted abortions.[59] Complications from a botched abortion is one of the five leading causes of women's death in Honduras.[60] One of the most common means of birth control is sterilization—which many women have done without consulting their mates.

Legal protections against sex discrimination are not well developed and only rarely enforced in Honduras. As the last Latin American country to grant women the right to vote (in 1954), Honduras has taken only limited steps to protect the rights of women. Single childless women have no adjudicative land rights, whereas all males over 16 years of age have such rights. When a landowner dies, his land passes directly to his oldest son — not to his widow, unless otherwise arranged. The country's penal code exempts husbands of culpability in cases of assault, battery, and even murder if his wife is caught in an adulterous act.[61] Only in 1984 did the country's Family Code give rights to children born out of wedlock, an important step in enforcing paternal responsibility.

Women Organizing

Honduras has a long and proud history of women organizing for their rights.[62] The Women's Culture Society, founded in 1923, was the nation's first women's organization. With close links to the communist-led Honduran Union Federation, the society led the fight for political and economic rights of Honduran women, with a special focus on the families of banana and mine workers. It sponsored educational seminars and published the *Cultura de la Mujer* magazine. Visitación Padilla and Graciela García, the society's two leading figures, were among the country's major popular activists. García, a Salvadoran, lived in Honduras until her expulsion in 1944 for her long history of opposing the Carías dictatorship (1933-1949).[63]

The Federation of Honduran Women's Associations was founded in 1950 to lead the fight for women's suffrage. Largely an organization of middle-class and professional women, the federation was instrumental in the institution of the country's Family Code and has a social-service program to promote organizing projects by poor women.

The Honduran Federation of Peasant Women (FEHMUC), founded in 1978, is one of the few female peasant organizations in Latin America. FEHMUC grew out of the rural Housewives' Clubs (CAC) within CARITAS, the Catholic church's social-service organization and the Social Christian peasant movement. Inspired by the "preferential option for the poor" tendency within the church, the CAC movement became increasingly active in social-justice issues. After the 1975 Olancho massacre and the mounting pressure against activist clergy, the Catholic church pulled back from many of its more committed social programs. At the same time, the more politically aware activists with the CAC were pushing to separate their community organizations from the Catholic church and affiliate with the National Campesino Union (UNC). Many of the women belonging to the CAC movement were the wives of UNC members.[64]

At a 1978 conference organized by ex-CAC leaders, FEHMUC was founded. By the late 1980s FEHMUC comprised 294 women's groups in 13 of the 18 Honduran departments. Its purpose is to integrate peasant women into the social, economic, and political life of the nation. For its social service and educational programs FEHMUC has received aid from the UN Voluntary Fund for Women (UNIFEM), the Inter-American Foundation (IAF), European foundations, CARE, PACT, and most recently from the U.S. Agency for International Development (AID).

Claiming that FEHMUC was becoming increasingly conservative and classist, a left-leaning faction split off in 1987 and founded the Council for Integrated Development of Peasant Women (CODIMCA). CODIMCA, which receives funding from progressive organizations in Europe, comprises some 100 women's groups which sponsor small development and social-service projects in Lempira and other departments. Among other things, it promotes the use of traditional herbal medicine.[65]

Another new women's organization is the Visitación Padilla Committee, named after the founder of the Women's Culture Society. Padilla, a leftist peace activist in the 1920s, co-founded the *National Defense Bulletin* which sparked popular opposition to the intervention of the U.S. Marines in Honduras in 1924.[66] The committee has protested the U.S. military buildup and contra presence in Honduras, and has petitioned that the National Congress pass a law that would establish severe legal penalties for violence against women.

The League of Patriotic Honduran Women (LIMUPH), founded in 1988, works in the poor urban *barrios*. Other organizations include the Center of Women's Studies which associated with the Liberal Party; the Association of University Women; and another organization of professional women called the Committee for the Defense of Women's Rights (CLADEM). Prior to the 1989 election, the Federation of Honduran Women's Organizations (FAFH) expressed concern that the presidential candidates were ignoring the country's socioeconomic problems, which they said indicated a deep contempt for the Honduran people.

Ethnic Groups and Native People

To a large degree Honduras is an ethnically homogeneous society— the population being about 90 percent *mestizo*, or mixed Indian and Spanish. The remaining population is made up of 7 percent pure Indian,

2 percent black, and one percent Caucasian.[67] Spanish is the national language although English Creole and Carib and Mayan dialects are also spoken. In the Bay Islands, La Ceiba, and other areas along the Atlantic coast there is a small black population which speaks English and English Creole. The main settlements on the island of Roatán, for example, are predominantly black. The Bay Islands also are inhabited by whites, some of whom claim to be descendants of Henry Morgan and other English pirates. These Antillean whites migrated to the Bay Islands in the 1830s from the Caribbean islands. There are also small communities of Arabs and Lebanese (deprecatingly called *turcos*) which play a major role in the country's business and industry.

The Garífuna or Black Caribs

Honduras has two different black ethnic groups. The Antillean blacks, who live on the North Coast and the Bay Islands, are descendants of laborers imported from Belize, Caiman Islands, and Jamaica to work on the banana plantations. Along the Atlantic coast and in the Bay Islands there are also communities of Garífuna, also known as Black Caribs. These are descendants of African slaves who were either shipwrecked or runaway slaves and found refuge among the Carib Indians in Saint Vincent, an island of the Minor Antilles. Eventually these blacks became the dominant ethnic group on the island, and their own culture and language became mixed with those of the Carib Indian. There was also interbreeding, but not as much as was formerly believed.[68]

Considered "troublesome savages" by European colonizers, the French and later the English attempted to return them to slavery. Strong Garífuna resistance made this free population difficult to subdue but they were eventually rounded up in the 1790s and taken to Roatán. Within a few years the Spanish colonizers allowed the Garífuna to come to the mainland where they helped rebuild the port of Trujillo which had been burned down by pirates. Soon the Garífuna extended their settlements along the Caribbean coast from Belize to Costa Rica. There are some 70,000 Garífuna living in Honduras, most of whom are very poor.[69] The Black Fraternal Organization (OFRANEH) represents the interests of the Garífuna community.

The Amerindians

The indigenous population at the time of the Spanish conquest has been calculated at about 800,000, although other estimates rise as high as 1.4 million or more.[70] Even before the conquest, the Maya civilization was in decline. The magnificent Copán religious and political center had been abandoned before the Spanish arrived. Estimates of the the current Amerindian population in Honduras range from 157,000 to 450,000.[71]

Disease, massacres, work in the mines, and the Spanish slave trade were among the leading causes for the rapid decline of the native population. Some 30,000 to 50,000 Indians were killed during the conquest while tens of thousands of others later died from disease.[72] Leading the main resistance to the Spanish incursion was the Lenca chief Lempira, who was finally killed in 1539.

As many as 150,000 Indians, particularly those living along the coast, were enslaved and exported to estates and mines in Guatemala, the Caribbean islands, Nicaragua, Panama, and Peru. Not wishing to have their children born into such circumstances, Indians apparently induced miscarriages and practiced infanticide as well as abstention from sexual intercourse.

There are two general groups of Honduran Indians: the settled agricultural communities of the west and the aboriginal Indians of the northern lowlands. Of the former group, the most important tribe is the Lenca, and the others are the Chorti, Chorotega, and Pipil Indians. Although most speak Spanish, they still retain cultural and religious traits that set them apart from the dominant *mestizo* population.[73] The Pipils, living mainly in the isolated northern region of La Mosquitia and in Olancho and Yoro, are sometimes called the Forest Indians. They include the Miskito, Pech (Paya), Sumo, and Jicaque (Torpán) tribes. Because they are so isolated they are less acculturated than those living in western Honduras.

The Lenca inhabited the greater part of central Honduras at the time of the conquest, and today number about 50,000, concentrated in Intibucá, Lempira, and La Paz. The Chorti, a lowland Maya group, occupied the departments of Copán and Ocotepeque but migrated to the northern coast in the 17th and 18th centuries. Today the Chorti are almost extinct.[74] The Chorotega migrated south from Mexico to flee repression by the Olmecs and settled in Choluteca.

The Pipil Indians came to Honduras in the 9th and 10th centuries, about the same time as the Chorotegas. The Forest Indians are related to the South American rainforest peoples. The Miskitos, numbering over 35,000, are the largest group of forest Indians. Located in northeastern Honduras and across the border in Nicaragua, these Amerindians remained outside Spanish influence because of their isolated location.

The nearly 25,000 Miskito people of Honduras did not emerge as a distinct cultural-linguistic group until the mid-1600s. Closely related to the Sumu Indians, the Miskito people seemed to have been originally found near Cabo de Gracias a Dios and then spread along the coast, displacing Pech and Sumu communities. Like the Miskitos, the few remaining communities of Sumu Indians have been disrupted by the contra war. Many now live in temporary camps in Nicaragua and Honduras and it is feared that they may not survive as a people.[75] To avoid harassment, the Sumu people have abandoned their language and there are now less than 1,000 ethnic Sumus — divided into two subgroups, the Ulua and Tawahka. Most are subsistence farmers living along the Patuca River, and none have more than a sixth-grade education.[76]

At the time of the conquest the Pech are believe to have inhabited as much as one-fourth of Honduras, but they now number from 700-1,800 and are confined to a few small communities in Olancho, Colón, Gracias a Dios, and Yoro. The Pech have fought against having the national educational curriculum imposed on them and now have Pech language courses and Pech teachers. The Pech have also battled against land-grabbing by *mestizo* colonists and the National Agrarian Institute (INA).[77] There is also a small group of Jicaque Indians still living in Yoro.

Ethnic Organizing

Indian people in Honduras have been organizing on a national level since the 1950s. One of the first organizations was the Autonomous Ethnic Organized Movement of Honduras. Other organizations have been the National Federation of Tribes for the Liberation of the Honduran Indian (FENATRILIH) and the Unity Committee of Indigenous People (CUPIH). Groups like FENATRILIH, founded in 1978, aimed to improve the economic, political, and social conditions of the Indian population with a special emphasis on protecting Indian lands and facilitating agricultural credit and technical assistance, while other organizations have attempted to form a national federation of all Indian people that would be politically active. More recently the Garífuna have been included in national organizing efforts.

Many of the issues that concern the Indian tribes as well as other ethnic minorities were discussed at the Third National Encounter of Ethnic Peoples in 1988. The conference, which brought together representatives from most Indian tribes and Garífuna communities, demanded that the national government provide greater assistance to ethnic communities especially in the areas of health care, education, and the building of rural access roads. At the same time the ethnic groups represented at the conference stressed the importance of maintaining their culture, they also demanded that the government develop an immediate plan of action for the "total integration of this population into national life."[78] The conference also called for a law by which "members of indigenous communities, as well as the Garífuna, be protected against political and religious intolerance, against socioeconomic exploitation, and racial discrimination."[79] The principal coordinating organization for ethnic groups is the Honduran Advisory Council for Autonomous Ethnic Development (CAHDEA). Other individual groups include OFRANEH (Garífunas and other blacks), FETRIXY (Jicaque), ONILH (Lenca), MASTA (Miskito), FITH (Tawahka/Sumu), and FETRIPH (Pech).

Refugees and the Internally Displaced

Honduras is largely a host country rather than a source of refugees. Nicaraguans, Salvadorans, and Guatemalans have also sought refuge in Honduras from the wars in their countries. Increasingly, however, Hondurans are leaving the country, mainly for economic reasons but also because of increased human rights violations. One indication of this is the increasing number of Hondurans who are seeking political asylum in the United States.[80]

Hondurans Flee the Contras

A little-known result of the contra war in Honduras was the displacement of some 22,000 Hondurans from small villages near the Nicaraguan border.[81] The small border village of Jacaleapa in the department of El Paraíso was one of the first affected. The rise of crime and violence persuaded many villagers to leave their homes. Recognizing that a problem existed, U.S. ambassador John Negroponte gave a $25,000 check to CARITAS (charitable agency of Catholic church) to care for the displaced but blamed the problem on Sandinistas aggression.

By 1984 at least 14 villages had been abandoned as frightened and angry Hondurans left the border area. The newly displaced blamed the contras for their exodus. "We haven't been able to live in peace for five years," said one group. "We lost everything, and we aren't about to lose our lives and our children too. We cannot denounce these events because they accuse us of being Sandinista collaborators but the contras are the responsible party."[82]

In 1986 the contras declared part of El Paraíso to be "New Nicaragua," and counted on the close cooperation of the Honduran military. Groups of displaced Honduras began to make demands of the U.S. and Honduran governments. Some demanded the expulsion of the contras while others wanted to be relocated in another region. In early 1987 one such group called the Committee of Displaced from the Border Territories invited President Azcona to visit the area to verify that their claims about abandoned villages were not exaggerated.

As a result of the intensifying pressure and publicity, the U.S. Agency for International Development (AID) began providing development and relief funds to the displaced. Food-for-work programs were initiated for displaced families, and special aid went to the thousands of displaced small coffee growers of the region. Other groups like CARITAS, CRS, and the Red Cross also began programs to assist the displaced. As part of the regional peace talks Honduras has requested that the United Nations undertake programs to assist and relocate those displaced by the contras.

Central American Refugees

Honduras, on the border of three countries in war, has been a country of refuge for Guatemalans, Salvadorans, and Nicaraguans. Approximately 60,000 refugees were under the care of the United Nations High Commission on Refugees (UNHCR) by the mid-1980s. The winding down of the contra war and mass repatriations of Salvadorans resulted in a steadily decreasing refugee population in the late 1980s. In addition to those refugees with official refugee status, Honduras is host to an estimated 250,000 undocumented Central Americans—many of whom are war refugees.[83]

Guatemalans began spilling over into Honduras in the early 1980s when the country's counterinsurgency campaign was most fierce. At first the fleeing Guatemalans, mostly Indians from Alta and Baja Verapaz, sought refuge in the homes of Hondurans. Later the UNHCR established a refugee camp called El Tesoro near the Guatemalan border. Many Guatemalans have since returned home, although nearly 400 remained in Honduras as of 1989.[84]

Salvadorans have been pushed in and out of Honduras by war, poverty, and political tensions. During the 1960s some 200,000 Salvadorans homesteaded in Honduras but most were driven out of the country during the period leading up to the 1969 "Soccer War" between the two countries. Another source of tension between Honduras and El Salvador has been disputed border territory along the frontier of the Salvadoran department of Morazán.

In 1980 thousands of Salvadorans began fleeing into Honduras to escape the rampaging Salvadoran army and the intensifying civil war. In Honduras the Salvadoran refugees found refuge in UN-sponsored refugee camps. In cooperation with the UN, several local and foreign private organizations have administered these camps, including Catholic Relief Services, CARITAS of the Santa Rosa de Copán diocese, Honduran Mennonite church with volunteers from the Mennonite Central Committee, Medicins san Frontieres, and an evangelical relief and development agency called CEDEN.

Salvadorans in Honduras have been under constant military siege by the Honduran army. Upon entering the country, refugees have been killed by the Honduran military which, despite longstanding tensions between the two countries, has participated with the Salvadoran military in joint operations against the FMLN guerrillas and their supporters. The refugee camps in Honduras have been under tight military siege. On several occasions Honduran troops have entered the camps, brutalizing or killing refugees. Refugees in Colomoncagua charged that they have been victims of a "policy of persecution, psychological warfare, and assassinations."[85] Medicins san Frontieres has called the refugee camps "concentration camps."[86]

Beginning in 1987 Salvadoran refugees began repatriating. Receiving only a bare minimum of assistance from the Honduran government's refugee agency CONARE and the UNHCR, the refugees themselves organized several large repatriations, with many returning to their original communities in El Salvador. After a large repatriation in February 1990, there were only 6,000 Salvadorans still living in refugee camps in Honduras— many of whom were also planning to repatriate.[87]

Although there was little evidence that the Salvadoran refugees were FMLN guerrillas as the Honduran and Salvadoran military claimed, the Salvadoran refugees were highly politicized. Visitors to the camps were amazed at the degree of organization and collective spirit that the Salvadorans have promoted within the camps.

In contrast with the heavily controlled Salvadoran refugee camps, the Nicaraguan camps have been under little or no military control by the Honduran government. The camps have served as recruiting grounds for the contras and homes for the families of contras. Meetings of the contra leadership with U.S. military advisers took place openly in the camps. Many refugees, however, were not contra supporters and have since 1987 been part of a steady stream of repatriating Nicaraguans. Following the UNO victory in February 1990, the contras, their families, and other Nicaraguan refugees faced increased pressure to return to Nicaragua. But given the precarious economic conditions and continuing revolutionary/counterrevolutionary tensions, it is likely that Honduras will continue to host, willingly or not, many thousands of illegal residents from Nicaragua.

Environment

The long disregard for the environment has created an ecological crisis in Honduras—the consequences of which are just beginning to be understood. In the south, desertification is well underway and may be irreversible. The combination of wood cutting and unsustainable agricultural practices, particularly in the cotton and cattle industries, have denuded vast sections of southern Honduras. The result has been decreasing rainfall, falling agricultural yields, and widening food shortages. In the rush to exploit the nation's forest reserves, roads have been bladed into tropical forests, opening up these areas not only to clear-cutting but to colonization by land-hungry peasants and the abusive cattle industry.

Although Honduras is not heavily populated, its land resources are limited. Mountains traverse most of the country, and the soil is not enriched with the volcanic ash like in neighboring El Salvador. Rapid population growth—about 3.5 percent annually—is complicating the already serious land-use and land-tenure problems. By the year 2000 Honduras, with over 7 million inhabitants, will be facing the kind of population pressure already seen in El Salvador and Guatemala.

Honduras is slowing waking up to the environmental crisis, but there is still little environmental control. Honduras, for example, still serves as a regional export platform for parrots and other exotic wildlife. The few cloud forests in Honduras continue to disappear at a rapid pace. And the Honduran landscape is already so denuded that there is little hope for Honduras to cash in on the booming international eco-tourism business.

Deforestation

Deforestation is not a new problem. When Hurricane Fifi struck in 1974 landslides on denuded slopes along the Caribbean coast buried entire villages, leaving some 12,000 dead. Forest cover in Honduras decreased from 63 percent in 1960 to 36 percent in 1980—and the country continued to lose 3.6 percent of its remaining forests annually in the 1980s.[88] Most of the primary hardwood forests that once covered parts of Honduras are now gone, replaced by a secondary growth of pine.

Today even this thin cover of pines is threatened by rapid deforestation. At the current loss rate, the mature pine trees will be completely gone in ten years; all the country's woodlands will vanish in 20 years.[89] "Few stop to think that trees are more than simple sources of tables or fuel," said Francisco Martínez, project coordinator of the Honduran Association for Ecology. "The woods are water, climate, protection for the soil, forest life, tourism, and life."[90]

Cattle ranching, the timber industry, peasant colonization, and forest fires are among the main causes of this rapid deforestation. According to an archaic homesteading law, ranchers are given title of land they clear and graze. A powerful and reactionary sector, the large cattle ranchers have forced small farmers off the land and blocked all attempts at regulation. Cattle ranchers also regularly pay landless peasants to clear forested lands to make room for future pastures.

The timber industry is, however, the major culprit. Beginning with the British and then the entry of U.S. investors into the country's lumber industry, Honduras' forestry resources have long been exploited with little consideration for the long-term consequences of deforestation.

In 1974 the government nationalized the forestry industry as part of General López Arrellano's reform program. The stated purpose of the reform was to wrest control over the forestry industry from foreigners and a few local industries and to develop the country's woodland resources for benefit of the entire nation. Trees were nationalized, although not the land they stood on, with timber cutting subject to government license. The government also established a monopoly of the export of sawn wood. Although bitterly resisted by private sawmill owners, the Forestry Development Corporation of Honduras (COHDEFOR) was created and several giant publicly owned sawmills were constructed, including CORFINO in Olancho, FIAFSA in Yoro, and CASISA in Siguatepeque.[91]

But the reform of the forestry industry did not yield the desired results. As with other public-sector investments in Honduras, the public was the net loser. Environmental destruction actually increased as vast new areas were opened up to exploitation, and lumber exports increased but no corresponding forestry management program was put into practice. Development loans from international lenders like the Interamerican Development Bank (IDB) were for new road construction into forest reserves and for the construction of sawmills rather than for forestry management.[92] Licenses were granted to private lumber companies which took only the best wood, leaving more than half of the cleared forests to rot on the ground.

It was not, however, the quickening pace of deforestation that sparked new pressure to privatize COHDEFOR but the notorious corruption and inefficiency of the state enterprise. Between 1977 and 1985, COHDEFOR's investment program absorbed 10 percent of the increase in the country's external debt. Rather than a source of income, the state's forestry industry was a drain on the government's financial resources. The

U.S. Agency for International Development (AID) has insisted that COHDEFOR and its associated sawmills be privatized—a process that has already begun.

Although COHDEFOR has been corrupt, inefficient, and careless about the environment, there is little reason to believe that a privatized forestry industry will do much better. Many say that, given the exploitative history of private sawmills, the pace of environmental destruction will only increase because of the privatization program. Wood exports have been privatized, the sawmills are being sold off to private investors at tremendous losses, and COHDEFOR has relaxed its licensing system. Now private sawmills are being given exclusive control over tributary areas (partitions of forest land). Cutting quotas are still in effect but are commonly being ignored in the rush to increase exports and to meet the rising domestic demand for lumber.

Rigoberto Neza of the Honduran Association for Ecology complained that COHDEFOR is not enforcing the management plans stipulated in the tributary area agreements between loggers and the governments.[93] And according to Rafael Alegría of the CNTC rural association which includes many of the country's forest cooperatives, "Tributary areas amount to no more than the privatization of the forest."

Privatization has been a boon to the private sawmills and the investors who are buying up the large pulp mills and sawmills at bargain prices. One aim of privatization is to improve the product quality and delivery times of the country's lumber exports, with a view toward maintaining a competitive position in the increasingly competitive Caribbean market. Another objective is to cut government financial losses, although even after the privatization is completed the government will be left with more than $240 million in external debt payments accumulated by COHDEFOR.

Stumpage fees—the charge levied on private cutters—are quite low, about one-quarter of U.S. levels. These are scheduled to rise, but the lumber producers are notorious for their avoidance of government charges—from stumpage fees to income taxes and export levies. Aside from better enforcement of present controls on private producers and development of a stringent forestry management program, to increase the benefits of the country's lumber industry Honduras needs to increase the value of its wood exports by expanding its manufacturing industry. Currently, however, manufactured wood exports are only a minor part of total lumber exports.

Among those private investors moving in on the country's newly privatized forestry industry are former U.S. Assistant Secretary of State

Elliot Abrams and General Paul Gorman, former chief of the U.S. Southern Command. As partners in a lucrative new lumber corporation called Aerolift, Abrams and Gorman are planning to use sophisticated air transport to extract hardwoods from inaccessible Honduran forests.[94]

Ravages of War

Honduran militarization, U.S. military maneuvers, and the contra war are other causes of environmental destruction. Contra occupation of the border area in the department of El Paraíso have displaced some 16,000 Honduran families. According to the regional COHDEFOR office, the contras are pillaging the area's environment — cutting wood for their camps and profiting from contraband lumber sales to Honduran lumber mills and tobacco farms.[95] U.S. environmental groups including the Environmental Policy Institute and Environmental Project on Central America have protested the use of U.S. "humanitarian aid" to buy chainsaws and sponsor chainsaw safety training courses for the contras. In a letter to Congress, the groups stated that "U.S. money could be more appropriately spent on reforestation efforts and to restore land that has been destroyed through U.S. military training and other support for the contras."[96]

Frequent U.S. military maneuvers in Honduras have also contributed to deforestation. Fires from shooting exercises and construction of airstrips, roads, and military bases led one COHDEFOR official to charge that the 1986 maneuvers destroyed 10 percent of the pine forests in the savannahs near the Nicaraguan border.[97] Congressional hearings revealed that over a thousand square kilometers of the Honduran forest were deforested in the late 1980s as a result of U.S. military maneuvers and construction.[98] Other damage comes from the road-building by military engineering teams conducting civic-action operations in isolated areas of Yoro, Olancho, and other departments. These roads open up new areas of the country for exploitation, and as one U.S. Army spokesperson said, these construction projects are "less environmentally constrained. If you're building a road, you don't have to worry about the width of the culverts, about the EPA, or about the environmentalists. Those are not concerns down here."[99]

Agriculture, Ranching, and Pesticides

Honduras is cursed with some of the poorest land in Central America. The country is largely mountainous but lacking the rich volcanic earth of Costa Rica, El Salvador, and Guatemala. Its tropical lowlands in the east are characterized by thin soils, and only 31 percent of its hillside lands have deep fertile soil — compared with 76 percent in El Salvador. Only 11 percent of the land in Honduras is capable of supporting intensive annual crops, another 9 percent is suitable for perennial crops and pasture, and 13 percent is only capable of supporting perennial crops and forest plantation.[100]

Land-tenure and land-use patterns result in intense pressure on this limited productive land base. The best lands are in the hands of a narrow group of large growers, who often leave their estates uncultivated or dedicate these fertile lands for pasture. According to the latest land-tenure statistics, 4 percent of the country's landowners control 56 percent of the farmland. This skewed land ownership pushes peasant farmers onto the worst lands and toward the uncultivated but forested agricultural frontiers.

The environmental impact of agroexport crops vary. The traditional method of coffee cultivation, where the coffee bushes are placed next to shade trees, causes only limited environmental damage. By contrast, more intensive production currently being promoted by AID, where shade trees are removed and agrochemical use is increased, is more environmentally damaging. The increase of cotton production since the 1950s has been particularly damaging because of the large quantities of pesticides applied.

The use of DDT is still widespread in Honduras and high levels of DDT residues have been found in the fat tissues of those Hondurans living in Choluteca and other areas of southern Honduras.[101] A 1981 study in Choluteca, a rice and cotton region, showed that 10 percent of those living in the area showed high levels of intoxication.[102] In 1989 at least 129 Hondurans died from pesticide poisoning. Each year Honduras imports about $22 million in pesticides, but only 15 percent of the country's farmers receive any form of technical assistance in the proper use of these chemicals.[103] Not only are pesticides deadly for farmers but the country's food supplies have been found to carry high concentrations of these agrochemicals.

A related problem is the increase of malaria and dengue fever in coastal areas as mosquitoes become resistant to pesticides. Pesticide poisoning is an economic as well as a human problem. Because of the unregulated and high use of pesticides in Honduras, exports of beef and nontraditional crops like melons have been repeatedly turned back at U.S. ports.

About 30 percent of Honduran land is currently dedicated to cattle ranching, including much of its limited fertile farmland.[104] Foreign-aid programs, including those of the U.S. Agency for International Development (AID) encourage the growth of this industry, despite its contribution to the country's serious deforestation and erosion problems. Because of the low quality of Honduran soils, cattle require more grazing land than in other Central American countries. The stocking rate in Honduras is .65 cattle per hectare (about 2 1/2 acres) contrasted with a 2.36 rate in El Salvador.[105] The best beef is shipped to the United States while the stringy beef and less desirable body parts are left for the local market. Many restaurants in Honduras, however, advertise that their beef is of "export quality."

The spread of cattle across the Honduran landscape is a major factor in the country's declining per capita grain production. To meet the increasing demand for basic grains from the country's rapidly increasing population, small farmers have cleared new land. There were important gains in productivity made in the 1960s but these have largely been lost in the past two decades as the quality of the soil declines.

Over-fishing also has had negative environmental and economic consequences. The conch population, for example, has been so depleted that there is no longer enough conch for either commercial exploitation or local consumption. The lobster and shrimp industries have also been severely affected. Honduran fishermen earn the ire of Belizeans for their practice of killing the endangered manatees in Guatemalan and Belizean waters and selling the meat of these large aquatic mammals in the Honduran market.

Urbanization and Colonization

Evidence of the worsening circumstances in rural Honduras is found in the teeming slums of Tegucigalpa. Honduras is experiencing the most rapid urbanization rate in Central America — with the percentage of urban population rising from 18 percent in 1950 to 40 percent in 1985.[106] Forty years ago the capital was a quaint town of 75,000. Today there are over one million people living in this jungle of traffic jams, high crime, and human desperation. The pine-clad hills that once surrounded the capital city have long since been stripped bare to make room for tens of thousands of wooden shacks. For the most part, these hovels lack basic water and sanitation services. Electricity is generally available but few can afford the monthly charges. A survey by the National Water and Sewer Service found that of the 392 neighborhoods in Tegucigalpa, 219 are considered "marginal" because of their lack of basic services.[107]

Less than a third of the city's population has drinking water within their homes, and the rank-smelling Choluteca river is the only sewage system for many. There is a booming water-for-sale business in Tegucigalpa in which containers of water of questionable quality are sold to desperate slum dwellers. Shifting cultivation, road-building, and deforestation is undermining the nearby Los Laureles watershed and causing a rapid build-up in sedimentation in the reservoir that provides the city with 60 percent of its drinking water. Elsewhere in the country, the two new hydroelectric projects under construction — El Cajón and El Níspero — are already suffering from erosion problems related to the deforestation of surrounding watersheds. Floods are another related problem. The peak runoff from steep watersheds is estimated at 10 times more than when the mountains were heavily forested.[108]

The environmental problems caused by urbanization are not confined to Tegucigalpa. Contamination of the Chamelecón and Blanco Rivers, which pass through San Pedro Sula, has polluted water supplies in surrounding villages and departments. Skin ailments are common among the poor who are obligated to wash their clothes and bathe in these rivers. Most of the contamination comes from the many factories that are located inside city limits and dump their refuse into the rivers.[109]

Another mainly urban problem is air pollution from motor vehicles. Medical authorities have concluded that 60 percent of the reported respiratory illnesses are due to exhaust fumes.[110]

The rapid pace of urbanization and its consequent problems reflect the increasing number of landless and land-poor peasants who are leaving rural areas. The other side of this problem of landlessness is the alarming rate of colonization of previously uninhabited regions, including the arid highlands and tropical eastern lowlands. The government has encouraged and at times aided this colonization process in the hope of defusing rural unrest. But the spread of hungry peasants into isolated forested areas is contributing to the country's deforestation as land is cleared for farms and pastures and fires consume additional acres.

National Parks and Environmentalism

Honduras was the last country in Central America to establish a national park system. The Tigra Cloud Forest near Tegucigalpa was created in 1979. The country's other major park, the Copán National Park which protects the Mayan ruins near the Guatemalan border, is administered separately from the newly created national park system.[111] The government has proposed placing 6 percent of the national territory into protected reserves but only some two-thirds of that has actually been designated as reserve lands.

The Río Plátano Reserve, one of the few reserves created, has suffered as a result of the contra war. "Perhaps the most troubling news,"

concluded a 1988 COHDEFOR report, "is that the contra war is destroy-
ing the Río Plátano zone." With the influx of Nicaraguan Miskito
refugees, the reserve's human population doubled at the height of the war.
Also a threat is a proposed road that would connect Puerto Lempira and
Tegucigalpa.[112] In the works is the Biotopo Trifinio international reserve
on the Honduras-El Salvador-Guatemala border. This project, aside
from being a reserve, would also be the site of numerous development
projects, including proposed mining projects.[113]

Environmental consciousness is expanding in Honduras. One of the
new environmental organizations formed in the 1980s is the AID-funded
Honduran Association for Ecology, which promotes its visionary project,
"Toward a Green Honduras in the Year 2000." Probably more important
in the long run, however, is the rising environmental consciousness among
popular organizations like peasant associations which are now including
environmental protection issues along with their other concerns and
demands. The most combative and progressive environmental group is
the Committee for the Preservation of the Fauna and Flora of the Gulf of
Fonseca (CODEFFAGOLF). Among other projects, it is organizing displaced and threatened communities along the gulf to protect their lands
and mangrove forests from the depredations of new shrimp-farming ventures involving foreign capital and corrupt military figures.

Chapter 5

Foreign Influence

U.S. Foreign Policy

It was not until the Sandinista victory in 1979 that Honduras was placed high on the list of U.S. foreign-policy priorities. But even before its rise to geopolitical importance Honduras existed in the shadow of Washington. During the first half of this century U.S. diplomats looked after the interests of the two U.S. banana companies, United Fruit (United Brands) and Standard Fruit (Castle & Cooke), which accounted for over 80 percent of Honduran exports. To ensure that U.S. lives and property were adequately protected, U.S. warships were sent to Honduras several times in the the early 1900s and U.S. troops occupied the capital city in 1924.

U.S.-Honduran Relations 1954-1980

After World War II, U.S. foreign policy broadened as Washington began to take a more active interest in the course of Latin American politics and economy. In the 1950s the Pentagon began shaping the Honduran military into a strong national institution capable of playing a leading role in national politics and repressing leftist dissidence. The new dimensions of U.S. foreign-policy interests in Honduras became apparent after 1954 — a watershed year in Honduran politics and society.

Foreshadowing its role as a platform for U.S. militarization of the region, Honduras in 1954 allowed its territory to be used as a training ground for the CIA-supported rightwing military force that overthrew the reformist government of Jacobo Arbenz in Guatemala. The same year Washington signed a bilateral-assistance pact with the Honduran military that laid the foundation for the close U.S.-Honduran military cooperation of the 1980s. It was also during the banana strike in 1954 that U.S. labor representatives associated with the State Department began infiltrating the Honduran labor movement and exerting the conservative, anticommunist influence that has long obstructed the advance of a unified, progressive popular movement in Honduras.

During the 1960s and the 1970s the Pentagon continued to be the main source of foreign support for the Honduran armed forces. On the economic front, the U.S. Agency for International Development (AID) provided grants and loans for the construction of hydroelectric dams, highways, rural roads, farm credit, agroexport promotion, public administration, grain marketing, private enterprise promotion, and public administration. Backed by U.S. funds and supplies, nongovernmental organizations like CARE, the American Institute for Free Labor Development (AIFLD), and Partners of the Americas began operations in Honduras.

Prior to the late 1970s there was little U.S. pressure for Honduras to move from military to civilian rule. Suddenly, however, U.S. hegemony in Central America was threatened by the the Sandinista challenge to Anastasio Somoza of Nicaragua and the rise of leftist movements in Guatemala and El Salvador. Bordering all three countries, Honduras gained new strategic importance for Washington. It soon came to occupy a pivotal position in U.S. policy towards Central America.[1]

The outlines of U.S. foreign policy became apparent soon after the Sandinista victory in July 1979. Secretary of State for Inter-American Affairs Viron Vacky presented a major policy report to Congress in September 1979 in which he pointed out that "Honduras' geographical position gives it a key role in preventing regional conflicts and potential infiltrations." Even before the ouster of Somoza, however, the Carter administration had begun to pay closer attention to political stability of Honduras. In 1978 the State Department began working with the military junta led by General Policarpo Paz to facilitate a transition to civilian rule in 1980.

Instituting a policy that later would be repeated in El Salvador and Guatemala, the Carter administration adopted a dual program of political reform and militarization. With an election schedule in place and the promise of the military to cede direct control of the government to the political parties, the United States stepped up its commitment of economic and military aid to Honduras in 1980.[2] To bolster the Honduran military's capacity to patrol the Nicaraguan and Salvadoran borders, the Carter administration loaned the Honduran Air Force ten Huey helicopters. At the same time the U.S. Southern Command (SOUTHCOM) sent a Special Forces team to Honduras to instruct the armed forces in border security operations.[3]

The Carter administration moved quickly to help Honduras adapt to its new geopolitical role. It pushed through a provisional agreement in October 1980 to settle the long-running border dispute between Honduras and El Salvador. This agreement provided for joint border patrols and granted the Salvadoran army access to the pockets of disputed of border territory (known as *bolsones*) where Salvadoran guerrillas were camped. The expanding cooperation between the two armies had severe consequences for the thousands of Salvadoran refugees fleeing into Honduras. In one bloody incident some 600 Salvadorans were killed, mostly by Honduran troops, as they attempted to cross the Sumpul River into Honduras. Besides taking an active role in the Salvadoran conflict, the Honduran armed forces were also pressured by the United States to patrol the Nicaraguan border to prevent the alleged smuggling of weapons through Honduras into El Salvador.

Foreign Policy during Reagan Era

The Carter policy of political reform seasoned with generous doses of militarization established the foundation for massive injections of military and economic aid by the Reagan administration. Like Carter, President Reagan recognized that a civilian government in Honduras was essential to the credibility of U.S. claims that its main foreign-policy goal in Central America was to shore up democratic governments. Under Reagan the strategic significance of Honduras increased as the country became the launching ground for the Nicaraguan contra war. In the early 1980s the role assigned to Honduras in the regional crisis expanded from containment to counterrevolution.[4] The U.S. diplomatic corps, rising to over 1,300, was one of the largest in the world.

Assistant Secretary of State Elliot Abrams said: "Our political objectives for Honduras are clear: to strengthen democracy and democratic institutions, to elicit full cooperation against nondemocratic forces in the region, to encourage regional cooperation and solidarity, and to obtain the greatest Honduran support possible for our objectives in the region and elsewhere. Our economic objectives must bolster and reinforce our overall objectives which can and would be undermined if political and social progress is not achieved."[5]

In the 1980s U.S. foreign policy did succeed in eliciting Honduran cooperation for its program of counterrevolution and militarization. During the decade Honduras received over $1.6 billion (1980-1989) in direct U.S. military and economic aid. Largely as the result of this aid, Honduras became, as President Suazo had once reminded President Reagan, Washington's "closest ally" in Central America.

The interdependence between the two countries deepened during the 1980s. Large sums of U.S. economic assistance kept the economy afloat, and large allocations of U.S. military aid kept the armed forces acquiescent in the face of the "democratization" process and the expanding contra presence. For its part, Washington relied on Honduras for close cooperation in its war of destabilization against Nicaragua. Honduras had also become a base for a U.S. military buildup — having allowed the Pentagon to construct an extensive infrastructure of air fields, bases, and radar sites in the country.

This interdependent relationship is likely to continue in the 1990s. With the apparent termination of the contra war and the electoral victory of UNO in Nicaragua, the country lost much of its immediate geopolitical importance for Washington. But the threat of leftist challenges in El Salvador and Guatemala, the continuing strong presence of the Sandinistas in Nicaragua, and the valuable military infrastructure put in place during the 1980s make it likely that Washington will remain committed to maintaining Honduras as a base for regional operations and intervention for many years to come.

Strains in the Alliance

The alliance between Honduras and Washington was strained during the 1980s by Honduran demands for still more assistance. As the political and social costs of the contra and U.S. military presence rose, Honduran leaders became less grateful for the proffered aid and more convinced that the country was not receiving a fair shake. In exchange for allowing Honduran territory to be used in carrying out the United States' dirty work, Honduras repeatedly demanded a higher rent. There were no second thoughts about selling the country's sovereignty for U.S. aid, but Honduran government and military officials became increasingly unhappy with what they were getting back in this shameful *quid pro quo* deal.

Growing popular and official resentment about the imperial ways of Washington rose to explosive proportions following the U.S. arrest of Honduran drug kingpin Juan Ramón Matta. During a student protest march in April 1988, the U.S. embassy annex was attacked and set afire with the apparent complicity of Honduran security forces. Students were outraged that the United States had once again violated Honduran sovereignty, while forces within the military and police were apparently angered by new U.S. initiatives to interfere with the country's profitable drug trade. In 1987 the U.S. Drug Enforcement Administration (DEA) had reopened its office in Honduras which had been closed in the early 1980s — apparently as a favor to the military high command.

The occupation of Honduras by U.S. troops met little opposition during the first half of the decade. This began to change in 1986 following the U.S. airlift into Honduras of 3,200 rapid deployment troops in response to a Nicaraguan offensive against the Honduras-based contras. Increasingly, popular organizations began to call for the removal of U.S. troops and bases, while media commentators and politicians expressed concern that the country's dignity and sovereignty were being trampled upon by the United States. Increasingly, U.S. troops became the target of bombings and ambushes. Most of the attacks were either claimed by the country's small guerrilla groups or blamed on them. Significantly, however, the U.S. embassy did not dismiss the possibility that it was the Honduran military that was the responsible party in at least one bombing.

The alliance faces a rocky future in the 1990s. Budget constraints, the fading Cold War, the Sandinista electoral defeat, and a rising chorus of funding demands from Nicaragua, Panama, and Eastern Europe will all make it more difficult for Washington to find sufficient funds to keep Honduras content in its role as a platform for U.S. military ventures in the region. Total U.S. aid is expected to decline and as this flow of dollars slows, nationalistic and anti-U.S. tensions will sharpen.[6] These tensions will be also aggravated by the austerity measures and currency devaluation that the Callejas administration is likely to impose as a result of U.S. and IMF pressure.

U.S. Policies Destabilize

Democracy, development, and stability have been the oft-repeated U.S. goals in Honduras. But after ten years of aid and intervention, these goals still seem distant. In fact, rather than moving Honduras forward, U.S. policies and programs in Honduras appear to have sown the seeds of economic and political instability. This failure can be attributed in part to the contradictory and misdirected character of U.S. economic and military assistance. But it also has to do with the fact that from the beginning Washington's interest in Honduras has been mainly a product of U.S. foreign-policy concerns in Nicaragua, El Salvador, and Guatemala.

At the same time that Washington voiced its support for democratization, it proceeded to militarize the country by fortifying its army and police, occupying it with U.S. troops, and establishing a counterrevolutionary army. The result has been that Honduras has become an increasingly repressive and polarized country and a civilian government rules in the shadow of a military that is stronger than ever.

The provision of economic aid has been largely counterproductive. Large injections of balance-of-payments assistance did temporarily ease the financial crisis but resulted in Honduras become an aid junkie increasingly dependent on the foreign-assistance fix. Instead of directing funds to programs that would address the basic needs and development concerns of the poor majority, AID favored the elite private sector with U.S. dollars. (See U.S. Economic Aid) While corrupt colonels, politicians, and businessmen soak up the U.S. aid, the socioeconomic conditions for the majority of Hondurans have markedly declined.

Attracted to Honduras because of its lack of internal political turmoil, Washington proceeded to support the military and the business elite, while obligating the government to adopt political and economic positions contrary to the interests of the workers, peasants, and middle class. In so doing, the United States has shaped a more polarized and repressive nation and contributed to the country's long-term instability.

The Bush administration seems determined to repeat and extend the mistakes of the previous administration. Rather than backing away from a one-sided commitment to the private sector, the new administration has deepened this commitment, with the U.S. embassy openly allying itself with the Council on Private Enterprise (COHEP) and the narrow business interests of the National Party.[7]

The designation of Cresencio Arcos as the new U.S. ambassador to Honduras also signaled a continuation of U.S. policy in Honduras. Arcos served in Honduras as the director of the United States Information Service (USIS) under ambassador John Negroponte, the U.S. official who directed the militarization of Honduras and the buildup of the contra army. Arcos, a career diplomat, later served as the deputy director of the Nicaraguan Humanitarian Aid Office which oversaw the delivery of nonlethal assistance to the contra forces.

U.S. Trade and Investment

Honduras has long been a country dominated by the economic presence of the United States. The banana plantations of Standard Fruit (Castle & Cooke) and United Fruit (United Brands) have been dominating factors in the Honduran economy since the late 1890s. More than simply a banana republic, Honduras has also attracted U.S. investors and traders in mining, manufacturing, services, and diversified agricultural production.

Ninety percent of the foreign investment in Honduras is from the United States.[8] The United States is also the country's leading trading partner — supplying 39 percent of its imports and purchasing over 50 percent of its exports.[9] The leading exports to the United States are fruit (bananas and citrus), coffee, seafood (shrimp), vegetables, and beef. Honduras buys machinery, agricultural chemicals, and basic grains from the United States.

The book value of U.S. investment in Honduras is estimated to be $250 million, and the top three investors are United Brands, Castle & Cooke, and American Pacific Mining.[10] Close to 300 U.S. companies do business in Honduras, including 60 of the top 500 corporations in the United States.[11]

All three major U.S. banana companies have operations in Honduras. While United Fruit and Standard Fruit's plantations date back almost one hundred years, RJ Reynolds (Del Monte) is a newcomer to the banana business. Castle & Cooke, owner of Standard Fruit, also produces pineapples and African palm oil and is experimenting with the production of winter vegetables. United Brands has African palm estates and cattle ranches in addition to its banana plantations.

The top three U.S. banks — Citicorp, BankAmerica, and Chase Manhattan — conduct business in Honduras. Citicorp has interests in Banco de Honduras while Chase Manhattan owns part of Banco Atlántida. In the manufacturing sector, Kimberly-Clark makes toilet paper, Beatrice Foods produces snacks, Sterling Drug manufactures pills, United Brands produces plastics and vegetable oil, and Castle & Cooke is the country's major beer and soft-drink processor.[12] Among the other major industries dominated by U.S. investment are oil refining (Texaco), mining (American Pacific/AMAX), beef and poultry production, insurance, shrimp cultivation, and animal-feed production. The industrial parks in Puerto Cortés and Choloma, Cortés have attracted a score of U.S. manufacturers, including Christian Dior, which produce apparel and other goods for the U.S. market.

Because of their domination of certain economic sectors, U.S. corporations have been able to exact extraordinary concessions from the government. The banana companies have repeatedly threatened to lay off hundreds of workers or completely close down operations if the government did not lower export taxes. On one occasion in 1984 Standard Fruit agreed to retain 500 workers who had been threatened with layoffs after the government agreed to suspend its tax collections for one year and not insist it pay past property taxes.[13] A similar agreement was signed with United Brands.

The U.S. companies also use their economic leverage to break unions. Standard Fruit tried to break one union by switching its pineapple production to another corporate subsidiary. AMAX, the corporate giant that owned Rosario Mining, closed down its operations in 1987 to break the union, opening up a half a year later under the administration of another subsidiary called the American Pacific Holding Company. The "new" mining firm was eligible for a series of incentives and tax breaks that AID had pushed through to encourage foreign investment. During its first 18 months, six Honduran miners died because of unsafe working conditions. A new workers' union charged that safety problems arose after the former union was destroyed by the shutdown and corporate shuffling.[14] Texaco, the country's only refinery, has also used its monopoly position to force the government to keep taxes low and prices high.

Pressured by AID, the Honduran government has increased the incentives offered to foreign investors in the 1980s. Designed primarily to stimulate nontraditional export production by foreign investors, new measures include partial or total exemption from export taxes, the right of foreign investors to hold dollar-denominated accounts in the country, and easy capital repatriation. Honduran capitalists resent the privileged place given U.S. investors and succeeded in reducing major tax breaks that were suggested in the 1989 foreign investment law supported by AID.

Honduran businesses have also resisted U.S. efforts to liberalize all foreign trade. AID insists that trade liberalization (dropping all tariff barriers) would make Honduran industry more competitive but local businessmen have protested that an increasing influx of foreign goods is killing domestic industries. Not only do new consumer products threaten local businesses but used clothing and shoes from the United States are flooding into the local market.

Most new U.S. investment in Honduras has been attracted by the provisions of the Caribbean Basin Initiative (CBI) and assorted U.S. government programs to promote export production. Several new business-promotion organizations funded by AID, including the Foundation for Investment and Export Development (FIDE) and the National Council to Promote Exports and Investment (CONAFEXI), offer generous lines of subsidized credit and marketing assistance to companies exporting to the United States. As a result of these efforts, U.S. imports of apparel from Honduras more than doubled and total U.S. imports of manufactured goods increased by 90 percent between 1983 and 1988.[15]

U.S. Economic Aid

During the 1980s Honduras ranked among the top ten recipients of U.S. economic assistance in the world. Well over half of this aid has come in the form of Economic Support Funds (ESF) for balance-of-payments support. Between 1981 and 1990 Honduras received $711 million in ESF, $370 million in development assistance, and $152 million in U.S. food aid. Not only did Honduras experience an unprecedented influx of economic aid during the 1980s, but for the most part this aid came in the form of direct grants rather than loans. Between 1984 and 1988 over 85 percent of U.S. economic aid consisted of grants, while grants had composed only some 30-40 percent of the economic-aid package in previous years.

The U.S. Agency for International Development (AID), which dispenses all this aid, has placed itself in a central position in the Honduran society and economy.[16] At first glance, no sector of the society seems untouched. Everyone and every organization appears to be on the AID dole. Political parties, judges, military/civic action teams, business associations and businessmen themselves, journalists, unions, development groups, charitable organizations, churches, cattlemen, and, of course, government ministries and ministers depend on regular AID handouts.

As pervasive as AID seems to be in Honduras, the positive developmental impact of these dollars is difficult to find. Socioeconomic conditions continue to worsen, the economy shows few signs of stabilizing, and the gap between the rich and poor has widened. This absence of development is not surprising, given the focus and objectives of the AID strategy in Honduras. Waste and corruption have also been a major problem in Honduras. Jaime Rosenthal, a former vice president under Azcona, charged that 30 percent of U.S. economic aid was lost to corruption and 50 percent was misdirected, going to the business elite rather than to programs to help the poor.[17]

The rush of AID funds into the country came not as a response to Honduran poverty and underdevelopment but as part of U.S. political and military goals in the region. As such, this aid has been a payoff for Honduran acquiescence to U.S. foreign-policy strategy for Central America.

AID has not used its economic-aid package to help Honduras tackle its deep structural problems such as land tenure patterns and declining per capita grain production. Nor has it insisted that the government and oligarchy develop strategies to meet the basic health, educational, and income needs of the country's impoverished majority. Instead AID has concentrated on implementing the macroeconomic and private-sector solutions that aggravate and accentuate the deep social and economic divisions in Honduras.

To win good will for the United States and soften the dislocations caused by its stabilization program, AID has spread a small portion of its development assistance to the popular sectors including some NGOs, women's organizations, unions, and peasant groups. But here too AID has ignored the real development and educational needs of these sectors. Instead the agency has focused on bolstering the most conservative popular organizations with nonconfrontative projects that stress individual and export-oriented solutions. Ignored are the more progressive and representative popular organizations that emphasize community-based and structural solutions to the country's pressing socioeconomic problems.

AID has not only deepened the country's economic dependency but has also further debilitated the country's governmental and nongovernmental sectors. Through its agricultural, health, educational, finance, and other development programs, AID has created a "shadow government" in Honduras. Outside consultants have been placed in most ministries; and the government has become accustomed to turning to AID and the U.S. embassy for consultation and approval of most economic and political decisions. The same U.S. influence and control has come to pervade the nongovernmental sector as well—from the smallest social-service organizations to the country's largest business associations. Washington has bought friends and immediate influence and has established structures and operating methods that guarantee that Honduras will remain the type of society that Washington wants—irrespective of which individual politicians, bureaucrats, and businesspeople come and go.

The Pace of Economic Stabilization

Over half of U.S. economic aid to Honduras during the 1980s has been in the form of Economic Support Fund (ESF) grants, which are primarily used to relieve the country's foreign-exchange crunch. Honduras qualifies for such a large commitment of ESF aid because the Pentagon and the State Department (both of which sign off on ESF allocations) consider Honduras to be critical to U.S. security interests. The PL480 Title I food-aid program functions the same way in that it saves the country from using scarce foreign exchange to buy U.S. wheat.

At the same time that ESF and Title I ease the country's balance-of-payments crisis, they also provide the government and the private sector with a source of local currency to fund AID-approved programs. This secondary impact of the ESF and Title I food-aid programs works this way: private-sector importers and wheat mills use local currency (*lempiras*) to buy U.S. dollars and U.S. wheat from the government. This local currency is then divvied up among government ministries, private development groups, and AID itself, according to agreements AID makes with the government.[18]

Besides their value as balance-of-payments aid and as generators of local currency, ESF and to a lesser extent Title I assistance are used by AID to exact economic-policy reforms by the Honduran government. U.S. economic assistance comes with certain conditions, many of which are stipulated in the aid agreements themselves and others are hammered out in what AID calls "policy dialogues." Sometimes caveats come in the form of directives from the U.S. ambassador. Such was the case in late 1981 when Ambassador Negroponte handed the newly inaugurated President Suazo with a 12-point economic-stabilization program that was incorporated almost word-for-word into the new government's Plan of Action. Four years later the "Azcona Plan" for economic development was largely written by AID.

AID's formula for economic stabilization for Honduras has been the same package of neoliberal remedies the United States has been trying to impose on other third world countries. The plan's main components are privatization of state-owned enterprises, currency devaluation, budget cutbacks, liberalization of trade, and promotion of nontraditional exports. It is a plan that parallels the structural-adjustment programs that the International Monetary Fund (IMF) and the World Bank have been trying to institute in Honduras since the early 1980s.

The basic thrusts of AID's economic-stabilization plan are to impose austerity measures on the Honduran economy that will cut budget deficits and allow the government to meet its debt payments, and to place private investment in export production in the center of the country's development strategy. According to this strategy, once the economy is stabilized and exports begin picking up, the benefits of growth will trickle down to the poor. But as AID has acknowledged, "implementation of a stabilization program will probably lower living standards and may well increase unrest among the country's already impoverished people in the short term."[19]

AID has had mixed success in forcing Honduras to implement its stabilization plan. Austerity measures have been set in place and increased resources and incentives have been directed to the private sector. But as of early 1990 Honduras still had not devalued its currency, budget deficits remained high, and privatization had proceeded at a slower pace than AID has demanded.

Recognizing that full implementation of AID's stabilization measures would substantially increase the current level of social unrest, President Suazo and, to a lesser extent, President Azcona resisted AID pressure to devaluate the *lemipra* and reduce budget deficits. They were able to do this by playing off Washington's political and military strategy for Honduras against its economic one. It has been more important to the U.S. embassy that Honduras remain a compliant partner in U.S. militarization and support for the contras than that it fully comply with AID's stabilization demands. When AID has attempted to withhold further assistance, higher authorities in the Pentagon and State Department called for the release of that aid.

While AID probably will have more luck in pursuing its structural-adjustment remedies with the Callejas administration, Callejas will also hedge on AID and multilateral economic requests for fear of igniting popular unrest. Resistance to devaluation, tariff reductions, and austerity measures is also strong among many sectors of the business community which recognize that externally imposed economic stabilization plans might in fact drive the economy into a cycle of recession and inflation.

Private-Sector Support

Outside the government, the private sector is the favored recipient of AID funds.[20] The economic assistance goes either directly to business associations or to development and social-service organizations that sponsor private-sector solutions to social and economic problems. The business community is also the main beneficiary of AID-generated credit and of policy reforms stipulated in economic-assistance agreements with the government.

Nearly two dozen business associations and promotional groups receive AID funds, either directly as part of Development Assistance and ESF grants or indirectly from local currency generated by balance-of-payments support. Among the most important are the Honduran Council of Private Enterprise (COHEP), Federation of Agroexport Producers (FEPROEXAH), Foundation for Business Investigation and Development (FIDE), National Association of Honduran Exporters (ANEX-HON), National Association of Industrialists (ANDI), Associated Managers and Entrepreneurs of Honduras (GEMAH), National Development Foundation of Honduras (FUNDAHEH), and the Honduran American Chamber of Commerce (HAMCHAM). At least half of the business associations currently receiving support were founded by AID in the early 1980s.[21]

Other AID private-sector funding goes to such groups as the Cattle Fund (created by AID to promote beef exports), Honduran Foundation for Agricultural Research-FHIA (the former research department of United Fruit converted by an AID grant into a research center for banana, citrus, and nontraditional agroexport crops), and CADERH (AID-created vocational education center to train students to meet private-sector needs).

This devotion to private-sector solutions even extends to population control. AID is funding a Private Sector Population Program that is using the techniques of "social marketing" to sell and distribute birth control devices. AID is also funding the "social marketing" approach in the schooling and popular education through AVANCE, an elite AID-created organization. AVANCE sponsors radio programs, a newspaper, and other popular education ventures, and believes it can play a role in reforming the Honduran population by "fostering the values needed to make you efficient in your work and give you the capacity to create your own businesses and initiatives."

AID pressured the National Congress to adopt two measures—the Export Promotion Law of 1983 and the Temporary Import Law of 1984—to promote nontraditional exports and assembly manufacturing. But nontraditionals have failed to respond to new incentives.[22] During the 1980s most of the gains in the nontraditional agroexport sector were in palm oil and citrus—two products which are not supported by AID programs.[23]

Other examples of AID's extensive private-sector support programs include funding for an array of NGOs promoting microenterprises, backing of new export-processing zones, industrial parks, and initiatives to "strengthen the private forestry industry," and encouraging local and foreign investors to buy out state enterprises through its Privatization of State-Owned Enterprises Project.

In his evaluation of AID programs in Honduras, Philip Shepherd of Florida International University observed that AID "clothes its aid in the language of reform, broadly shared development, and democracy. This is either wishful thinking or cynical perversion of the English language." He concluded:

> The greatest obstacle to successful U.S. aid in Honduras is the elitist and reactionary nature of the U.S. aid program itself. U.S. aid is *not* being directed toward the majority of poor Hondurans. Instead both U.S. aid and other economic policies are serving to

prop up an increasingly creaky structure of incompetent, corrupt, and venal elites.[24]

Democracy-Strengthening Assistance

In the 1980s the U.S. government launched a new branch of economic aid called "democracy-building" or "democracy-strengthening" assistance. Funds for these democracy projects are channeled through AID and the National Endowment for Democracy (NED), a government-funded private organization founded in 1983. In Honduras the democracy-strengthening projects have ranged from managing the voter-registration and election process to training political leaders.

AID has funded virtually the entire electoral process in Honduras. It funds the National Registry of Persons and the National Elections Tribunal—the two institutions responsible for the registration of voters and management of the electoral process. The November 1989 presidential election was entirely paid for by U.S. taxpayers, including the paper for the ballots, the printing of the ballots, marking pens for the ballots, construction of voting tables, curtains for the voting booths, international observers, the election return system and monitoring center, and the labor to manage the elections.

AID not only paid for the mechanics of the election but also for the three-part civic-awareness campaign that preceeded the voting. There was a six-month general education campaign in 1988 "designed to raise the awareness of the public about the advantages of the democratic system." In 1989 AID sponsored a voter-registration campaign and a second education campaign, this one devoted to presenting "key issues and the presidential candidates' positions." Also sponsored were radio and television debates and newspaper summaries of candidate positions.[25]

For all the AID funding and hyperbole about free elections, the integrity of the November 1989 electoral process was undermined by a high rate of abstention (despite costly get-out-the vote drives) and a highly inaccurate voter registry. The failure of the government and AID to implement the proposed cleaning up of the voter registry resulted in post-election charges of manipulation and fraud by losing parties. Nonetheless, AID's sponsorship of the electoral process in Honduras put an international stamp of approval on the presidential election.

The country's judicial and legislative institutions have also been included in AID's democracy strengthening. Judges and legislators are being trained by AID consultants and are being provided with a wealth of written materials and information services. Although AID notes that the Congress and Supreme Court have been traditionally weak institutions, its institution-strengthening projects do not address or even mention the principal cause of their debility and lack of independence – the overriding power of the armed forces. Also considered part of AID's democracy program in Honduras is the Central America Peace Scholarships Program through which over 4,000 Hondurans will be schooled or trained in the United States by 1992.[26]

Another AID component is called Democratic Leadership Training. Through national leadership conferences and more specialized courses, AID has set out to influence the country's most powerful figures. According to AID: "Training services will be provided for all levels of political leadership, from local to national. The political leadership will also benefit from improved support services, such as information systems and improved administrative backup and support."[27]

AID's leadership-training efforts extend beyond the political parties to selected unions, women's organizations, media, peasant organizations, and business groups. Key members of these organizations are trained "to promote the diffusion of democratic principles into these organizations."[28] In accordance with AID's commitment to "develop human rights organizations," the agency has directed ESF local-currency funds to the governmental COINDEH created in 1987.[29] (See Human Rights) AID funds are also channeled through U.S. private organizations such as the Overseas Education Fund (OEF) and the American Institute for Free Labor Development (AIFLD) to conduct their own political education courses.

In addition to AID funding, AIFLD in Honduras receives NED funds for civic-awareness and political education among the country's union and peasant sectors. Other NED funding goes through the Republican Party's Institute for International Affairs to the Center for Economic, Political, and Social Studies in Honduras. The center drew up the policy platform of the National Party and sponsored a self-serving national radio program on the history of Honduras and the National Party.[30]

Peace Corps, Labor Unions, Humanitarian Assistance

Honduras hosts the largest Peace Corps program in the world. The some 380 volunteers work in health, education, agricultural, and business programs. One of the most ineffective and inappropriate programs is an adult education program in which the volunteers, most of whom are themselves just learning the language, teach reading and writing to illiterate adults. The Peace Corps programs are often coordinated with AID projects, particularly in small-business promotion.

In mid-1988 AID began a two-year $27 million humanitarian-assistance program to provide nonlethal supplies, medical services, and skills training for the contras. A major contractor for this program was the International Medical Corps, which has provided medical aid to the contras and their families.

The AIFLD, in addition to its previously mentioned NED funding, receives AID Mission support for its Honduran program. Since the 1954 banana strike U.S. organized labor in association with AID and the State Department have worked to exercise a conservative, pro-U.S. influence among Honduran workers and peasants. The main vehicle for this effort has been AIFLD since its creation by the State Department and the AFL-CIO in 1962. In Honduras AIFLD has worked through the National Association of Agricultural Workers (ANACH) and the Confederation of Honduran Workers (CTH). In recent years AIFLD's influence has been waning as Honduran peasant associations and labor unions, including ones that it funds, have grown more progressive.[31]

Rather than support efforts to unionize agricultural workers, AIFLD has focused on programs to encourage an "entrepreneurial approach" among individual small farmers.[32] AIFLD sends Honduran labor and peasant leaders to training courses in "democratic unionism" in the United States, Panama, and Israel, as well as sponsoring in-country political education and training seminars.

U.S. Military Aid

Following El Salvador, Honduras has been the leading recipient of U.S. military aid to Latin American countries in the 1980s. During the decade almost a half a billion dollars in direct military assistance and training was provided to Honduras. Military aid to Honduras has had more to do with the wars raging in neighboring countries, particularly Nicaragua and El Salvador, than with any security threat faced by Honduras. The aid has served as a payoff to the Honduran armed forces for their cooperation in U.S. counterrevolutionary efforts in Nicaragua and El Salvador.

Cooperation between the U.S. military and the Honduran armed forces dates back to the 1920s when U.S. advisers helped the country's air force. Warships were sent to Honduran ports in a show of U.S. strength and to "protect U.S. interests" in times of political turmoil, and in 1925 U.S. Marines marched into Tegucigalpa to sort out a presidential succession dispute. In 1934 the Military Aviation School was founded and a U.S. officer served as its first commander.

Prior to the 1950s the Honduran military had little sense of itself as a national institution. As a result of post-World War II efforts of the U.S. Department of Defense (DOD) to establish strong alliances with Latin American armies, the Honduran military began to professionalize. The country's first military academy was established in 1950 under U.S. tutelage. With the signing in 1954 of the Bilateral Military Assistance Agreement between Washington and Honduras, the professionalization and strengthening of country's military took rapid steps forward.[33] Military advisers were dispatched to Honduras and remained in the country at least through 1967.[34]

In the 1950s Honduran officers also began receiving training at U.S. Army School of Americas in the Panama Canal Zone. Between 1950 and 1961, 391 officers and 691 recruits received training in Panama.[35] Gaining a new sense of importance and strength, the armed forces took control over the government in 1956. The country was returned to civilian rule in 1958, but the coup marked the beginning of a central role for the Honduran military in the political and social life of the country.

Between 1946 and 1980 Honduras received a total of $32.6 million in U.S. military loans and grants. Beginning in mid-1980 U.S. military assistance to Honduras rapidly increased, rising from $4 million in fiscal year 1980 to a high of $77 million in 1984. According to the 1990 Department of Defense budget presentation:

> Security assistance to Honduras is a tangible demonstration of the U.S. commitment to the defense and development of this key ally. The military program is critical to modernizing the Honduran armed forces in order to provide a credible deterrent to the Sandinista threat. This assistance also contributes significantly to the professionalization of the armed forces, a crucial factor in strengthening of Honduran democracy. An important goal of security assistance is to promote respect for human rights through improved training.[36]

The rapid growth in U.S. military interests in Honduras in the 1980s was made possible by a 1982 amendment to the 1954 bilateral accord. The new agreement specifically allowed the United States to upgrade three major airfields and an unspecified number of smaller air strips. The agreement was expanded again in 1988 to allow the United States to build a major radar station on the North Coast. Under consideration by the Honduran government is a revised military agreement — the third protocol of the 1954 agreement — that would permit the United States to build permanent military facilities in the country that would be owned by Honduras but run by U.S. forces. The agreement would also allow U.S. aircraft and ships to enter Honduras without previous permission from Honduran authorities.

Components of U.S. Military and Police Aid

The three elements of the military assistance country program are: Foreign Military Sales (FMS), Military Assistance Program (MAP), and International Military Education Training (IMET). During the 1980s most U.S. military aid (89 percent) has been allocated under the MAP grant program. In 1990, however, the DOD switched its military assistance to the FMS sales program, but placed all the FMS under the category of forgiven grant rather than the usual concessional sales.[37] Even at a time when the contras were under international pressure to dismantle and the Nicaragua government was abiding by the regional peace accords, the DOD in its 1990 request said that continued large military-aid program was "critical to military modernization and professionalization to counter the Sandinista threat."[38]

During the 1980s the only Latin American country to receive more military training under the IMET program was El Salvador. The IMET program provided military education to 9,500 military officials in the United States and other locations from 1980 to 1989.[39] In addition to the IMET training at the U.S. Army School of Americas (in Panama and after 1985 at Ft. Benning, Georgia), Honduran troops are being trained by Mobile Training Teams (MTTs) of U.S. Special Forces (Green Berets) which enter the country for short periods to train entire units in counterinsurgency tactics and other military skills. MTTs have been working in Honduras since August 1981.[40]

Outside the three main categories of military aid (MAP, FMS, IMET), the Honduran military has benefited from an array of other U.S. military-aid programs. Under the Overseas Security Assistance Management Program, the United States stations military managerial personnel in Honduras. In the 1980s nearly $2 million was authorized each year for this management program.[41] Honduras has also benefited from DOD military construction grants which finance the construction and maintenance of foreign military bases. Once constructed, the base is turned over to the host country but the U.S. military retains access and perusal rights to the facility. In 1987 and 1988 over $4.1 million was spent each year for U.S. military construction in Honduras.[42]

In 1985 Congress authorized an exemption for Honduras and El Salvador from the prohibition of U.S. aid to foreign police forces. In Honduras, $2.8 million was authorized for the program to supply the Honduran Public Security Forces (FUSEP) and other national police with training, riot control gear, weapons, vehicles, and communications equipment.[43] Aid to the Honduran police has also been provided under the Anti-Terrorism Program, which is managed by the State Department's Bureau of Diplomatic Security. Other police training has been sponsored by the International Criminal Investigative Training Assistance Program (ICITAP) run by the U.S. Justice Department.

Other sources of military-related aid include the DOD's Humanitarian Assistance Program, Exercise-Related Construction (See Military Maneuvering), and Commercial Sales. In addition to acquiring U.S. arms through the MAP and FMS programs, Honduras also purchases arms commercially from U.S. exporters. During the 1980s these purchases ranged from a low of $0.9 million in 1987 to a high of $3.9 million in 1988.[44] The U.S.-guided militarization of Honduras has benefited from the joint military exercises that have occurred on Honduran soil since 1981. Equipment and weapons used during the maneuvers rarely return to the United States but were left for use by the Honduran military and the contras.[45]

The U.S. military-assistance program in Honduras is supporting the Honduran Force Modernization Plan—a plan to increase the strength and mobility of the Honduran armed forces.[46] Among the plan's specific objectives are developing an effective counterinsurgency capacity, bolstering the army's ability to patrol the Salvadoran border, and building a deterrent force for national defense. Extensive U.S. support has also been given for psychological operations, intelligence, and civil affairs. The most expensive component of U.S. aid has been DOD support for the Honduran air force. In 1987 the United States agreed to replace the country's Super Mystere jet fleet with the 12 highly sophisticated F-5 jet fighters.[47] The United States has also provided two C-130 transport aircraft for remote operations support and is upgrading the country's fleet of 15 A-37 aircraft.[48]

U.S. Military Facilities in Honduras

More than simply a recipient of generous U.S. military aid and training, Honduras in the 1980s became a U.S. military outpost. Newly constructed air bases, radar stations, and air strips are part of this U.S. military infrastructure. The Enrique Soto Cano Air Base (formerly Palmerola) outside Comayagua, constructed in 1983, is operated by the Honduran air force but functions as the nerve center of U.S. military operations in Honduras. Stationed at the huge base is Joint Task Force Bravo (JTFB), a contingent of 1,100 U.S. troops and about half that number of Honduran soldiers. JTFB, which is a joint U.S. Army and Air Force command, coordinates U.S. military operations as well as the joint operations of U.S. and Honduran forces. Excluding military salaries and expenses for intelligence missions that originate at the base, the yearly operating costs amount to $25 million.[49]

Besides overseeing the troop maneuvers within the Honduran borders, the Soto Cano air base coordinates reconnaissance flights over Nicaragua and El Salvador. JTFB also manages an extensive military/civic action program, including regular food-distribution and medical programs. As part of its educational outreach, local children are invited on base "to inspect the U.S. military's largest aircraft."[50]

Since the early 1980s the U.S. military has operated two major radar stations. At Cerro La Mole, between Tegucigalpa and Comayagua, there is a long-range early warning system purportedly erected to signal Hondurans of a Nicaraguan invasion. A second station was constructed in late 1983 during joint maneuvers on Tigre Island in the Gulf of Fonseca. In 1988 Washington signed a Mutual Cooperation Agreement with the Honduran government that opened the door for the construction of a still larger radar station on the North Coast. The control of drug smuggling in the Caribbean Basin is the justification for the construction of this major radar station.

Numerous airstrips, most of which have served the contras, have been built by U.S. military engineers along the North Coast and the Nicaraguan border. These airstrips, the most famous of which is El Aguacate, were built during joint military maneuvers but continue to be maintained by the U.S. military. Special congressional appropriations have permitted the expansion and maintenance of the large airfields at the air bases of Palmerola and La Ceiba.[51]

In 1983 the U.S. military established the Regional Military Training Center (CREM) on the North Coast near Trujillo primarily to train Honduran and Salvadoran soldiers. After two years of operation, CREM had trained 5,600 Salvadoran and 5,900 Honduran troops in addition to several dozen Civil/Rural Guard officers from Costa Rica.[52] The center was closed in June 1985 due to strong objections by the Honduran military command at having the Salvadoran military trained on Honduran soil. After CREM's closure the U.S. military adopted a new strategy of establishing national training in each country. The Honduran Military Training Academy (CAME) in Olancho was opened in 1988.

Military Maneuvering

Joint maneuvers with the Honduran military have been conducted since 1965, but the frequency and scale of these training exercises picked up in the 1980s. Using DOD general funds, the Pentagon launched a series of more than six dozen military maneuvers that brought tens of thousands of U.S. regular forces and National Guardsmen to Honduras. The maneuvers, according to the DOD, have the following broad objectives: 1) help develop Honduras' defenses; 2) improve readiness skills of U.S. forces in deploying overseas; and 3) demonstrate U.S. commitment to the democratic nations of the region.[53] In practice, these exercises trained U.S. invasion forces for the Central America climate and terrain and built up a military infrastructure along the Nicaragua border. A related objective was to provide an infrastructure of logistical support for the contras.

Three short maneuvers took place in 1981-1982 along the Nicaraguan border. Having succeeded in carrying out these limited maneuvers without raising serious objections in Congress, the U.S. Southern Command under newly appointed General Paul Gorman launched military exercises of unprecedented magnitude and duration beginning in 1983.[54] These began with the Big Pine II exercises that lasted six months.

After 1983 Honduras has experienced an almost unbroken series of joint maneuvers. Besides playing out invasion and defense strategy, the maneuvers were designed to militarize Honduras. As part of the military games and training exercises, a network of roads has been built, a series of airfields constructed, barracks erected, tank traps dug, radar stations established, and ocean ports upgraded.[55]

Troops from the United States have far outnumbered those Honduran soldiers who have participated in the maneuvers. On several occasions the U.S. troops in Honduras for maneuvers have assisted the Honduran military with national defense concerns. In 1982 U.S. advisers assisted Honduran counterinsurgency units in the pursuit and interrogation of captured Honduran guerrillas, including a U.S. priest who was part of the guerrilla force.[56] In 1985 and 1986 U.S. units in Honduras for maneuvers were called upon to ferry Honduran troops to the Nicaragua border to defend against a possible invasion. Then, in 1988, 3,200 U.S. troops were airlifted to Honduras to protect the country against a Nicaraguan invasion that never happened. This expeditionary force touched off cries within Honduras that the country's national sovereignty was being violated by the U.S. military buildup.

The U.S. military presence has not been without its human costs to the United States. Accidents and shootings between 1983 and 1990 resulted in the death of 47 U.S. servicemen. Several bombings, some claimed by leftist guerrillas, wounded at least three dozen U.S. soldiers, and dozens more have been seriously injured as a result of accidents.[57]

Winning Hearts and Minds: Civic Action

The Pentagon has long promoted military/civic action and nation-building programs as part of its military aid and training in Honduras. In the 1960s the U.S. military guided the establishment of a civil-affairs office within the military command and encouraged the army to take a more active role in the country's civil affairs through educational, infrastructure, and social-service projects. These programs combined "as a purpose and intended result the strengthening and continuance of the military role in the country."[58]

In the 1970s, on the heels of the U.S. experience in Vietnam, Pentagon support for civic action diminished. But with stepped up U.S. involvement in the region in the 1980s, civic-action programs once again came into vogue. Not only did the U.S. military renew its support for the Honduran army's civil-affairs division but it also mounted its own civic-action programs.

The U.S. military/civic action programs in Honduras are of two types: those sponsored year round by Joint Task Force Bravo and those programs that accompany joint U.S.-Honduran military maneuvers. The most common civic-action programs are road-building and medical care but they also include well-digging, the building of schools and clinics, and various distribution projects. The road-building projects are carried out mostly by National Guard engineers while the medical programs are the responsibility of a wide range of specialized Army and National Guard units.

The medical outreach programs include: Immunization Readiness Training Exercise (IMRETE), Medical Readiness Training Exercise (MEDRETE, formerly known as MEDCAPS), Dental Readiness Training Exercise (DENTRETE), Veterinary Readiness Training Exercise (VETRETE), and clinic services offered several times a week at the Soto Cano air base.[59] According to Major Bernard Eugene Harvey, the purpose of these medical programs, aside from the training value to U.S. medical personnel, is to make the U.S. military "presence as palatable as possible to the Honduran people."[60]

From its headquarters at the Soto Cano air base, Joint Task Force Bravo sponsors a wide range of programs, mostly in the areas surrounding the base. Typically a MEDRETE team is airlifted into a rural village, teeth are pulled, aspirin and anti-diarrheal medicine is distributed, and immunization shots are given to hundreds of Honduran peasants lined up to see the U.S. military doctors. These actions generally succeed in generating good will for the U.S. military. From a medical standpoint, however, the MEDRETE programs have been criticized for being one-time affairs that provide inadequate treatment and lack the necessary follow-up. The Pentagon has acknowledged this weakness and is attempting to remedy it with longer term medical projects.[61]

Besides the U.S.-sponsored military/civic action programs, the United States, both through DOD and the U.S. Agency for International Development (AID), since 1985 has been bolstering the Civil Affairs (C-5) capabilities of the Honduran military. The United States began "motivating the Honduran military to engage in Military Civic Action as part of a national development plan."[62] Under the tenure of General López, the military command sponsored a series of joint military and civilian seminars on civic-action programs.[63] Military Technical Projects (PROMITEC) was created to plan and execute civic-action projects and accompanying psychological operations.[64]

AID's Office of Disaster Assistance has supported new military initiatives in disaster assistance and civil defense, and has worked to reestablish the Permanent National Emergency Committee (COPEN), originally established by the military in 1975. COPEN, which coordinates disaster assistance and other civic-action programs, is directed by the chief of Civil Affairs. During the late 1980s, aside from from providing direct aid to COPEN, AID has supplied disaster assistance to the Honduran military for several programs along the Nicaragua border.

With U.S. support, COPEN and the Civil Affairs command have established a network of military-controlled civil-defense committees throughout the country. COPEN is the national coordinating institution, for regional committees known as CODERs and local civil-defense committees called CODELs. Both COPEN and Civil Affairs have received training from the U.S. Army's 361st Brigade of Military Civic Action. Supplies for the Honduran military's civic-action programs come from AID and U.S. private organizations, including World Opportunities International, Friends of the Americas, and Adolph Coors Brewery.[65]

Other Foreign Interests

Trade, investment, and aid from the United States far outweighs the influence of any other country. Japan, West Germany, and Italy are next in line among the country's largest trading partners. Israel, while not a large trading partner, has exerted substantial influence in Honduras through its military aid and agricultural-development programs. West Germany is the country's most important trading partner in Europe, and it has also been a reliable source of credit and loans. Honduras' inability to pay off past loans resulted in a suspension of West German loans to Honduras.[66]

Soviet interests in Honduras have been limited by the pervasive U.S. influence in the country as well as by the country's own disinclination to deal with the socialist bloc. This began to change in 1987 when Honduran government officials moved to set up trading relationships with the Soviet Union and Eastern Europe. Honduras has had some success in increasing its exports of coffee, bananas, and citrus fruit to the Soviet Union and Czechoslovakia.[67] The post-1987 expansion of trade with socialist bloc nations reflected the will of some Honduran business sectors to engage in commercial relations irrespective of ideologies.

Israeli Interests

Ties with Israel have largely been a by-product of the U.S.-Honduras alliance. Israel's primary role in Honduras has been one of arms distributor but it also has served as a source of highly sophisticated technological supplies. Israeli military expertise has been put to use training the military and the contras.

During the 1970s Honduras became a major client for the Israeli arms industry. In the late 1970s Honduras purchased a dozen Israeli-modified French Super Mystere fighter planes from Israel, making it the first nation with supersonic aircraft in the region.[68] Other arms purchases from Israel included: Arava STOL aircraft, a fleet of armored vehicles mounted with recoiless rifles, Galil rifles, and Uzi submachine guns.[69]

After a 1982 visit to Honduras by Defense Minister Ariel Sharon, arms and training for the Honduran army and air force increased. During the tenure of armed forces chief Alvarez Martínez, Israelis trained an elite counterinsurgency unit called the Cobras. Working out of the U.S.-operated Regional Military Training Center (CREM), more than a dozen Israeli advisers trained the Cobras and other military units. Israelis also trained the personal security guards of Honduran presidents Suazo and Azcona.[70]

Working closely with the United States and the Honduran military, Israel also has supplied military aid and training to the contras. According to some accounts, the link between the contras and Israel goes back as far as 1979 and was based on earlier contacts between Israel and the National Guard in Somoza's Nicaragua.[71] Israeli involvement in the 1979-1981 period of the contra war is unclear, but by 1982 the contras were reported to be speaking of Israel as an international supporter. In 1981 or 1982 the CIA had apparently entered into an agreement with Israel to supply Soviet bloc weapons to its covert war against the Sandinistas.[72] General Alvarez, who provided a conduit for the Israeli aid, was interested in establishing a larger Israeli operation in Honduras and may have suggested that the Honduran military and Israel take over the direction of the covert war.[73]

Reports of Israeli weapon deliveries to the contras southern front began to surface in 1983, with both Edén Pastora's ARDE (Revolutionary Democratic Alliance) and the FDN (Nicaraguan Democratic Force) benefiting. An arrangement had been made in the early 1980s with the CIA to supply Soviet bloc weapons captured from the Palestine Liberation Organization (PLO) in Lebanon to the then-covert contra operation.[74] When Congress in 1984 began to curtail U.S. support for the covert war, Israel increased its aid.[75] According to former U.S. mercenary Jack Terrell, Honduran officials received kickbacks every time the contras purchased weapons from Israeli arms dealers.[76]

Another facet of Israeli involvement in Honduras has been its agricultural-development programs. The Israeli government has sponsored agricultural-training programs and places technical consultants in various Honduran ministries. "For Israel, what is important," observed Jane Hunter of *Israeli Foreign Affairs*, "is to make known its agrotechnical products and to make friends, perhaps among them Honduras' future business and political leaders."[77]

Israel's military and economic interests have coincided in the nontraditional agroexport operations of Emil Sa'ada, "a major middleman for Israeli arms sales to the contras and owner of Shammesh Agrotech."[78] In the wake of the Iran-contra scandal, Sa'ada was identified as having run an "arms supermarket" linked to Colombian drug traffickers and as having served as a main conduit in Honduras of Israeli arms to the contras.[79]

Reference Notes

Introduction

1. For an excellent discussion of the limitation of the "formal democracy" in Honduras see: Mark B. Rosenberg and Philip L. Shepherd, eds., *Honduras Confronts Its Future: Contending Perspectives on Critical Issues* (Boulder: Lynne Rienner Publishers, 1986), pp. 22-53 and 230-234. Also see: Victor Meza, ed., *Honduras: Pieza Clave de la Política de Estados Unidos en Centro América* (Tegucigalpa: CEDOH, 1986).

2. Interview by Medea Benjamin, Food First.

3. The declarations of Judge Miguel Angel Izaguirre led to the creation of the Special Investigative Commission on Drug Trafficking (CIEN). *Boletín Informativo*, CEDOH, December 1989.

Chapter One

1. Jack Anderson, "Why Another Somoza?" *Washington Post*, 28 March 1980.

2. Richard Lapper and James Painter, *Honduras: State for Sale* (London: Latin American Bureau, 1985), p. 81.

3. Victor Meza, "The Military: Willing to Deal," in *NACLA Report on the Americas*, January-February 1988, p. 14.

4. *Central America Report*, 15 December 1989.

5. Unless otherwise cited, all material in this section is based on James A. Morris' excellent study of Honduran politics. See "The State and Elections" in James A. Morris, *Honduras: Caudillo Politics and Military Rulers* (Boulder: Westview Press, 1984), pp. 60-73.

6. Cited in Lapper and Painter, op. cit., p. 98.

7. *Los Angeles Times*, 30 November 1988.

8. More details on the history of Honduran political parties and their internal factions can be found in Morris, op. cit., pp. 74-78; Margarita Oseguera de Ochoa, *Honduras Hoy: Sociedad y Crisis Regional* (Tegucigalpa: CEDOH/CRIES, 1987), pp. 98-112; Lapper and Painter, op. cit., pp. 7-10; and "Elecciones Otra Vez," *Boletín Informativo*, CEDOH, October 1989, pp. 8-12.

9. "Un Cristiani para Honduras?," *Pensamiento Propio*, November 1989, p. 36.

10. "Falló el Acarreo a las Urnas," *Pensamiento Propio*, December 1989, pp. 2-3.

11. See "Un Cristiani para Honduras?" op. cit., p. 36.

12. Good accounts of the elections held in Honduras since 1980 can be found in Leyda Barbieri, "Honduran Elections and Democracy: Withered by Washington" (Washington: Washington Office on Latin America, February 1986), and Morris J. Blachman, William M. LeoGrande, and Kenneth Sharpe, *Confronting Revolution: Security Through Diplomacy in Central America* (New York: Pantheon Books, 1986), pp. 129-130 and 151-152.

13. This argument is developed in greater detail in Rosenberg and Shepherd, *Honduras Confronts Its Future*, op. cit., pp. 23-53 and 230-234.
14. *Tiempo*, 1 December 1981, cited in Alison Acker, *Honduras: The Making of a Banana Republic* (Boston: South End Press, 1988), p. 124.
15. *Boletín Informativo*, December 1989, p. 1.
16. For more details, see Lapper and Painter, op. cit., p. 81.
17. Details on the constitutional crisis of 1985 can be found in: Acker, op. cit., pp. 124-125; Lapper and Painter, op. cit., pp. 113-115; and *Central America Bulletin*, August 1989, p. 4.
18. For more details on the Pact of National Unity, see Oseguera de Ochoa, op. cit., pp. 148-150.
19. Accounts of the irregularities reported in the 1989 elections can be found in: *Central America Report*, 17 November 1989; *Regionews from Managua*, 1 October 1989 pp. 9-10; *Latin American Regional Reports*, 30 November 1989, p. 7; and "Falló el Acarreo a las Urnas," *Pensamiento Propio*, op. cit., pp. 2-3.
20. These declarations and further details on accusations of irregularities can be found in *Miami Herald*, 3 December 1989; *Latin America Regional Reports, Mexico and Central America*, 30 November 1989, p. 7; and *Inforpress Centroamericana*, 7 December 1989, pp. 15-16.
21. As a result of the 1989 elections the National Party candidates will occupy 73 percent of the municipal and mayoral posts, including Tegucigalpa and San Pedro Sula, and the party will have 71 representatives in Congress to the Liberals 55.
22. An outstanding analysis of the roots of Honduran foreign policy and the major issues confronting the country from 1975 to 1985 is Ernesto Paz, "The Foreign Policy and National Security of Honduras," in Rosenberg and Shepherd, *Honduras Confronts Its Future*, op. cit., pp. 181-209.
23. Cited in ibid., p. 197.
24. Cited in ibid., p. 219.
25. Cited in ibid., p. 220.
26. The most blatant example of this was the unconstitutional installation of the CREM, a base set up in Honduras by the United States in 1983 for training Salvadoran troops.
27. For more information on APROH, see Rosenberg and Shepherd, *Honduras Confronts Its Future*, op. cit., p. 187; Lapper and Painter, op. cit., pp. 101-102; and Scott Anderson and John Lee Anderson, *Inside the League* (New York: Dodd, Mead, and Co. Inc., 1986), pp. 217-241.
28. Cited in Lapper and Painter, op. cit., p. 110.
29. For details on the 1969 war and its aftermath, see Morris, op. cit., pp. 110-113.
30. One good account of the issues surrounding contra demobilization is Joseph T. Eldridge, "Honduras Left to Push Contra Pram," *The Nation*, 29 May 1989.
31. See Oseguera de Ochoa, op. cit., pp. 86-89.
32. *Censa's Strategic Report*, Number 11, June 1988.
33. *Miami Herald*, 13 January 1989.
34. *The Nation*, 29 May 1989, p. 736.
35. *Honduras Update*, October 1987, p. 2.
36. *Central America Report*, 19 August 1988.
37. Excerpts from the text were reproduced in *Boletín Informativo*, July 1988, p. 13.
38. Americas Watch, "Human Rights in Honduras: Signs of the 'Argentine Method'," December 1982, pp. 5-6.
39. *Boletín Informativo*, October 1984, cited in Acker, op. cit., p. 122.

40. Meza, "The Military: Willing to Deal," op. cit., p. 16.

41. For one account of the court proceedings, see Americas Watch, "Honduras: Without the Will," 1989, pp. 69-77.

42. See "A Death Squad Defector's Story," in Americas Watch, "Human Rights in Honduras: Central America's Sideshow," 1987, pp. 126-143. The defector's exposition includes a wealth of information on the methods used by Battalion 3/16, its links with the CIA and contras, the location of clandestine jail cells, and the Honduran officers involved.

43. Americas Watch, "Honduras: Without the Will," op. cit., pp. 2-3.

44. In fact, by the time the Azcona government left office in early 1990, the agreed date for payment of damages had already passed and the families had not received anything.

45. Cited in *Our Search*, ACAFADE, March 1989.

46. Americas Watch, "Central America's Sideshow," op. cit., p. 64.

47. Americas Watch, "Honduras: Without the Will," op. cit., pp. 59-60.

48. See *Miami Herald*, 14 November 1989, and U.S. Department of State, *Country Reports on Human Rights Practices for 1988* (Washington, February 1989), pp. 610-622.

49. Americas Watch, "Honduras: Without the Will, op. cit., p. 8.

50. CODEH, "The Situation of Human Rights in Honduras: 1988" (Tegucigalpa, February 1989), p. 12.

51. Americas Watch, "Honduras: Without the Will," op. cit., pp. 1-2.

Chapter Two

1. Tom Barry and Debra Preusch, *The Central America Fact Book* (New York: Grove Press, 1986), p. 112.

2. For a comprehensive account of the military's role in Honduras during the 1980s, see Victor Meza, "The Military: Willing to Deal,"in *NACLA Report on the Americas*, January-February 1988, pp. 14-21.

3. Cited in Morris J. Blachman, William M. LeoGrande, and Kenneth Sharpe, *Confronting Revolution: Security Through Diplomacy in Central America* (New York: Pantheon Books, 1986), p. 135.

4. The lower figure is cited in *The Military Balance, 1988-1989* (London: The International Institute for Strategic Studies, 1989), p. 198. The higher figure was cited for 1988 in "Informe Especial: Distensión No Pasa por Centroamérica," *Inforpress Centroamericana*, 7 December 1989.

5. Cited in U.S. Embassy, "Handbook on Honduras: Democracy, Defense, Development, Diplomacy and Drug Control" (Tegucigalpa, Fall 1988).

6. Raúl Sohr, *Centroamérica en Guerra* (Mexico: Alianza Estudios, 1989), cited in *Inforpress Centroamericana*, 7 December 1989.

7. George Thomas Kurian, *Encyclopedia of the Third World, Third Edition* (New York: Facts on File, 1987). This source cites 25 combat aircraft, to which must be added the 12 F-5 fighters acquired in 1989. Total of 120 aircraft cited in U.S. Embassy, "Handbook on Honduras," op. cit.

8. U.S. Embassy, "Handbook on Honduras," op. cit.

9. See *NACLA Report on the Americas*, January-February 1988, p. 30.

10. For more details on the involvement of Honduran officials in international drug trafficking, see Jacqueline Sharkey, "The Contra-Drug Trade Off," *Common Cause*, September-October 1988, pp. 23-33; Eric Shultz, "Top Civilians Involved in Drugs,

Says Ex-Judge, with Military Backing," *Honduras Update*, June-July 1988, pp. 14-16; and *Central America Report*, 27 May 1988, p. 158.

11. Cited in "Honduras: A U.S. Base for Intervention" (Philadelphia: NARMIC/American Friends Service Committee, March 1989), p. 6.

12. The main sources consulted for the national-security doctrine and militarization in Honduras were: *NACLA Report on the Americas*, January-February 1988; *Honduras: Fuerzas Armadas 1988, Contrainsurgencia Interna y Disuasión Regional* (Mexico: Instituto de Investigaciones Socioeconómicas de Honduras, 1988); Margarita Oseguera de Ochoa, *Honduras Hoy: Sociedad y Crisis Regional* (Tegucigalpa: CEDOH/CRIES, 1987), pp. 53-63; and "Military Impact Indicators," *Honduras Update*, March 1987, pp. 1-3.

13. Richard Lapper and James Painter, *Honduras: State for Sale* (London: Latin American Bureau, 1985), p. 92.

14. *Boletín Informativo*, CEDOH, July 1989, p. 3.

15. See Rosenberg and Shepherd, *Honduras Confronts Its Future*, op. cit., p. 189, and *Honduras: A Country Study* (Washington: U.S. Government Printing Office, 1984), p. 236.

16. See Lapper and Painter, op. cit., p. 95, and Oseguera de Ochoa, op. cit., p. 59.

17. Lapper and Painter, op. cit., p. 94.

18. Ibid., pp. 101-102.

19. One detailed account of Alvarez' rise to power and his links to the Argentine military, the Moonies, and the World Anti-Communist League can be found in Anderson and Anderson, op. cit., pp. 217-241.

20. This included not only providing secure bases for the contras in Honduras and occasional military backup for contra incursions and retreats across the border, but also the direct participation of Honduran military personnel in attacks and sabotage operations inside Nicaragua. See "Military Insubordination," *Washington Report on the Hemisphere*, 21 January 1987.

21. *Tribuna*, 13 October 1984, cited in *NACLA Report on the Americas*, January-February 1988, p. 17.

22. For details on the current Honduran interpretations of national-security doctrine, see the text of a speech delivered by Regalado in January 1989 in "Seguridad Nacional y Conflictos Internos," *Boletín Informativo*, February 1989, pp. 6-7.

23. See *Boletín Informativo*, October 1989, pp. 4-5.

24. Cited in "Honduras Fears Contras Will Pose Security Threat," *Los Angeles Times*, 30 November 1988.

25. Accessible accounts of the activities of Battalion 3/16 include George Black, "Dirty Hands in Honduras: The Many Killers of Father Carney," *The Nation*, 23 January 1988; *New York Times*, 5 June 1988; and Julia Preston, "Honduras Accused of Death Squad Operations," *Washington Post*, 1 November 1988.

26. See Preston, op. cit.; and CODEH, "The Situation of Human Rights in Honduras: 1988" (Tegucigalpa, February 1989), p. 13.

27. See COHA, "12th Annual Report on Human Rights in Latin America," 25 December 1988, and "Surge la 'Triple A' en Honduras," *Boletín Informativo*, April 1988, p. 16.

28. See *News from Americas Watch*, March 1989.

29. See CODEH, "The Situation of Human Rights in Honduras," op. cit., and *Boletín Informativo*, April 1989, p. 4.

30. For more details, see Anderson and Anderson, op. cit., pp. 219-221.

31. See "Violence Triggers Diverse Responses," *Central America Report*, 4 August 1989, p. 237.

32. Cited in *Boletín Informativo*, March 1989, p. 14.

33. See Roger Burbach, "Restive Honduran Military, Ready to Bite the Hand that Feeds It," *Pacific News Service*, 23-29 January 1989, pp. 3-4.

34. Information on the following groups has been taken from Lapper and Painter, op. cit., pp. 9-10; Helen Schooley, ed., *Conflict in Central America* (Essex, UK: Longman Group Ltd., 1987), p. 165; and Oseguera de Ochoa, op. cit., pp. 139-142.

35. See *Central America Bulletin*, August 1989, p. 6.

36. See "Honduran Leftist Group Claims Bombing," *Washington Post* 16 July 1989.

37. For accounts of this incident, see "Mysterious Death of Father Carney," *The Nation*, 4-11 August 1984, and "The Many Killers of Father Carney," *The Nation*, 23 January 1988.

38. *Central America Report*, 25 August 1989, p. 261.

Chapter Three

1. The two most graphic examples of the dismal failure of this approach are CONADI, set up in 1974 to provide low-cost investment funds to the private sector, and COHDEFOR, the state's forestry development corporation. Today, both are in the process of being broken up and sold to private investors, local and foreign, and their massive debts have been absorbed by the government.

2. *Los Angeles Times*, 30 November 1988.

3. U.S. embassy reports on the investment climate in Honduras show no net growth in the amount of direct U.S. investment between 1982 and 1988.

4. *Tiempo*, 1 February 1989, cited in *Boletín Informativo*, CEDOH, February 1989, p. 2. Many investors cite regional political instability as a major disincentive to opening new businesses in Honduras.

5. Figures from Interamerican Children's Institute, cited in *Hondupress*, 22 August 1989.

6. Cited in *Honduras Update*, March 1987, p. 6.

7. *Economic and Social Progress in Latin America: 1989*, Inter-American Development Bank, p. 14.

8. *CEPAL Review*, April 1984.

9. The performance in the 1980s of Honduras' top four nontraditional exports, which together account for more than 25 percent of income from all nontraditionals, has been mixed: palm oil has grown substantially, pineapple and fruit conserves have increased modestly, and manufactured wood products have seen a dramatic decrease. Eva Paus, ed., *Struggle Against Dependence: Nontraditional Export Growth in Central America and the Caribbean* (Boulder: Westview Press, 1988), p. 125.

10. *Business Latin America*, 27 November 1989, p. 379.

11. This was reported at a COHEP-sponsored seminar on privatization held in June 1989. See *Central America Report*, 24 June 1989.

12. Agriculture employs 63 percent of the labor force, its share of the GDP is 27 percent, and agricultural products account for 58 percent of export revenues. See George Thomas Kurian, *Encyclopedia of the Third World, Third Edition* (New York: Facts on File, 1987), p. 855.

13. In 1988 some 59 percent of the population lived in rural areas, down from 65 percent in 1980 and 70 percent in 1974.

14. *Encyclopedia of the Third World*, op. cit., p. 855.

15. This information is taken from Honduras background material supplied to Peace Corps volunteers, 1985, pp. 15-17.

16. *Encyclopedia of the Third World*, op. cit., p. 855.

17. U.S. Agricultural Attache Report, #HO-9002, 4 April 1989, p. 25.

18. *Crónica*, 7 April 1988.

19. See Latin America Data Base, *Central America Update*, "Country Notes, Honduras," 15 December 1989.

20. U.S. Agricultural Attache Report, op. cit., pp. 5-6.

21. Food and Agricultural Organization, *Food Security in Latin America and the Caribbean*, June 1984; Tom Barry, *Roots of Rebellion: Land and Hunger in Central America* (Boston: South End, 1987).

22. U.S. Agricultural Attache Report, op. cit.

23. *Hondupress*,18 April 1989.

24. For a full treatment of the objectives and consequences of the U.S. food-aid program see: Rachel Garst and Tom Barry, *Feeding the Crisis: U.S. Food Aid and Agricultural Policy in Central America* (Lincoln: University of Nebraska Press, forthcoming).

25. Roger Norton and Carlos Benito, "Evaluation of the PL480 Title I Program in Honduras," Winrock International for AID-Honduras, 1987.

26. *El Heraldo*, 2 November 1988.

27. *Boletín Informativo*, November 1988.

28. For one good analysis of the agrarian-reform program, see Medea Benjamin, "Campesinos: Between Carrot and Stick," in *NACLA Report on the Americas*, January-February 1988, op. cit., pp. 22-30.

29. *Boletín Informativo*, May 1989, p. 5.

30. Cited in *NACLA Report on the Americas*, January-February 1988, op. cit., p. 28.

31. *Boletín Informativo*, special edition on 25 years of agrarian reform, September 1987.

32. *Envío*, August 1989, p. 17.

33. According to one author, 77 percent of credit goes to export crops and livestock, while only 13 percent goes to basic grains. See Mario Ponce, "Honduras: Agricultural Policy and Perspectives," in Rosenberg and Shepherd, *Honduras Confronts Its Future*, op. cit., p. 146.

34. *NACLA Report on the Americas*, January-February 1988, p. 30.

35. "El Modelo Asiático No Es una Solución," *Pensamiento Propio*, September 1988.

36. *El Heraldo*, 12 May 1989, cited in *Boletín Informativo*, May 1989, p. 5.

Chapter Four

1. H. Berger, *Union Diplomacy: American Labor's Foreign Policy* (1966), p. 364.

2. See Tom Barry and Debra Preusch, *AIFLD in Central America: Agents as Organizers* (Albuquerque: The Resource Center, 1990), p. 40.

3. For more information see: Benjamin Santo, *Datos para el Estudio del Movimiento Social Cristiano* (Tegucigalpa: Instituto de Investigaciones Socio-Económicas, 1981).

4. *Directory and Analysis: Private Organizations with U.S. Connections-Honduras* (Albuquerque: The Resource Center, 1988), p. 5.

5. *Boletín Informativo*, CEDOH, November 1988.

6. U.S. Embassy, *Foreign Labor Trends: Honduras* (Tegucigalpa: U.S. Department of Labor, 1987).

7. Robert H. Holden, "In U.S.-Funded Honduras, Misery Trickles Down," *National Catholic Reporter*, 1 December 1989.

8. Guillermo Molina Chocano, "Problemas de la Democracia en Honduras," in Mark B. Rosenberg and Philip L. Shepherd, eds., *Honduras: Realidad Nacional y Crisis Regional*, (Tegucigalpa: CEDOH, 1986), p. 38.

9. Other APU members include the COPEMH Defense Front, Black Fraternal Organization of Hondurans, Coordinating Block of Patronatos, Workers Union of the Institute of Professional Instruction, Housing Institute Union, Progressive Student Front-April 30, and the Industrial Packaging Union.

10. Two comprehensive accounts of Honduran trade unions are: Mario Posas, "El Movimiento Sindical Hondureño Durante la Década de los Ochenta," CEDOH Special Edition, No.44, October 1989; and Neale J. Pearson, "Honduras," in Gerald Michael Greenfield and Sheldan L. Maran, eds., *Latin American Labor Organizations* (New York: Greenwood Press, 1987), pp. 463-494.

11. For more information on this strike and on *solidarismo* in Honduras, see CEDOH Special Edition, October 1989, op. cit., pp. 11-13; and *Central America Report*, 9 December 1988, pp. 382-383.

12. Ministry of Public Education, cited in *Tiempo*, 14 June 1989.

13. National Census of Population and Dwellings, 1988, sponsored with the support of the UN Population Fund.

14. Ibid.

15. U.S. Agency for International Development, *Honduras: Country Development Strategy Statement FY1986* (Washington: AID, May 1984), p. 23.

16. Philip L. Shepherd, "The Honduran Economic Crisis and U.S. Economic Assistance: A Critique of Reaganomics for Honduras," unpublished manuscript, p. 170.

17. *Tribuna*, January 23, 1989.

18. Alison Acker, *Honduras: The Making of a Banana Republic* (Boston: South End Press, 1988), p. 100.

19. *Central America Report*, 1 September 1989.

20. Ibid.

21. U.S. Embassy, "Honduras," January 1, 1989.

22. Ibid.

23. Comité de los Periodistas de los Estados Unidos, *La Prensa Hondureña: Un Periodismo del Silencio* (Tegucigalpa: Escuela de Periodismo de UNAH, 1984).

24. Ibid.

25. Ibid.

26. Council on Hemispheric Affairs, *Survey of Press Freedom in Latin America 1985-1986* (Washington, 1986).

27. Ibid.

28. *Boletín Informativo Honduras*, February 1989.

29. *La Prensa Hondureña*, op. cit.

30. Information on USIS programs supplied to authors by USIA.

31. Rosa Morazán, "Malnutrition: The Child's Side of the Crisis," *Hondupress*, December 15, 1989; George Thomas Kurian, *Encyclopedia of the Third World, Third Edition* (New York: Facts on File, 1987).

32. Morazán, op. cit., citing UNICEF study.

33. U.S. Agency for International Development, *Congressional Presentation FY1990, Annex II, Latin America and the Caribbean* (Washington: AID, 1989).

34. *Tiempo*, 11 May 1988, quoting Minister of Health Rubén Villeda Bermúdez.

35. Medea Benjamin, "Hunger in Honduras," *Links*, NCAHRN, Spring 1987.

36. *Primer Censo Nacional de Talla en Escolares de Primer Grado* (Ministerio de Educación Pública, 1987).

37. Tom Barry, *Roots of Rebellion: Land and Hunger in Central America* (Boston: South End Press, 1987), p. 16, citing CEPAL and AID statistics.

38. *Tribuna*, 8 November 1988.

39. *Tiempo*, 11 May 1988.

40. Mary Jo McConahay, "Highest Incidence of AIDS in Region," *Pacific News Service*, 2 February 1988.

41. Ibid.

42. Ibid.

43. Sandra Avila and Luis Sierra, "War Without Bullets," *Links*, Summer 1987.

44. *Centroamérica Hoy*, 17 May 1989.

45. Dr. Carlos Godoy Arteaga, *El Sistema Unico de Salud y Seguridad Social* (Tegucigalpa: 1988), p. 9.

46. This section on religion is excerpted from *Directory and Analysis: Private Organizations with U.S. Connections-Honduras*, op. cit.

47. *Tribuna*, 21 August 1989.

48. For a history of the Catholic church in Honduras see: José María Tojeira, *Panorama Histórico de la Iglesia en Honduras* (Tegucigalpa: CEDOH, 1986).

49. Gustavo Blanco and Jaime Valverde, *Honduras: Iglesia y Cambio Social* (San José: DEI, 1987). The discussion of the trends within the Catholic church is drawn largely from this excellent work.

50. World Vision, "Analysis de la Realidad Nacional de Honduras," 1988.

51. Ibid.

52. *Directory and Analysis: Private Organizations with U.S. Connections-Honduras*, op. cit.

53. Acker, op. cit.

54. Melba Reyes, "Situación de la Mujer en Honduras," *Paz y Soberanía*, March 6, 1988.

55. *Encyclopedia of the Third World*, op. cit.

56. Elvia Alvarado with Medea Benjamin, ed., *Don't Be Afraid Gringo: A Honduran Woman Speaks from the Heart* (San Francisco: Food First, 1987).

57. Cited in Dolly Pomerleau, "Women in Honduras," *Honduras: A Look at the Reality* (Hyattsville, MD: Quixote Center, July 1984).

58. Reyes, op. cit.

59. Nancy Peckenham and Annie Street, "Women: Honduras' Marginalized Majority," in *Honduras: Portrait of a Captive Nation* (New York: Praeger, 1985).

60. *Hondupress*, 6 December 1989.

61. Reyes, op. cit.

62. Peckenham and Street, op. cit.

63. Ibid. See Graciela García, *Páginas de Lucha* (Tegucigalpa: Editorial Guaymuras, 1981).

64. Salley Yudleman, *Una Apertura a la Esperanza: Estudio de Cinco Organizaciones Femeninas de Desarrollo de América Latina y el Caribe* (Inter-American Foundation, c1988), p. 33-37.

65. *Directory and Analysis: Private Organizations with U.S. Connections-Honduras*, op. cit.

66. Peckenham and Street, op. cit.

67. *Encyclopedia of the Third World*, op. cit., p. 849.

NATIONAL WILDLIFE FEDERATION™

RRR94108

Congratulations!

You are now a Junior Member of National Wildlife Federation®. This great gift means you'll soon be receiving a full year of **RANGER RICK**® magazine. For cool activities and fun games exclusively for Junior Members, check out **www.nwf.org/rangerrick**.

This is a gift from:

Birgit Sharon

To:

Lewis Erickson

Please
Place
Stamp
Here

68. Ruy Galvao de Andrade Coelho, *The Black Carib of Honduras: A Study in Acculturation* (Evanston, IL: Northwestern University Press, 1955).
69. Melanie Counce and William Davidson, "Indians of Central America 1980s," *Cultural Survival Quarterly*, 1989, Vol. 13 No. 3, pp. 38-39.
70. Linda Newson, *The Cost of Conquest: Indian Decline in Honduras Under Spanish Rule* (Boulder: Westview Press, 1986).
71. The high estimate comes from the Consejo Asesor Hondureño para el Desarrollo de las Etnicas Autóctonas (CAHDEA), while the lower estimate was reported in Counce and Davidson, op. cit.
72. Newson, op. cit.
73. *Encyclopedia of the Third World*, op. cit., p. 849.
74. *Tiempo*, 4 July 1988.
75. Americas Watch, "The Sumus in Nicaragua and Honduras: An Endangered People," September 1987.
76. Ibid.
77. *Tiempo*, 16 July 1988.
78. *Tiempo*, 3 January 1989.
79. "Declaración de los Grupos Etnicos," *Boletín Informativo*, November 1989.
80. Of the 27,500 asylum requests processed by the U.S. Immigration and Naturalization Service (INS) in Texas during the last half of 1988, 11 percent of the applicants were Hondurans. *Washington Report on the Hemisphere*, 1 February 1989.
81. United Nations High Commission on Refugees, "Information Paper," International Conference on Central American Refugees, Guatemala City, 29-31 May 1989.
82. *Desplazados de Guerra Hondureños* (Tegucigalpa: CEDOH, October 1988).
83. January 1989 figures from United Nations High Commission on Refugees, op. cit.
84. U.S. Committee for Refugees, *World Refugee Survey: 1988 in Review* (New York, 1989).
85. *Central America Report*, 27 May 1988.
86. U.S. Department of State, *Country Reports on Human Rights Practices for 1988* (Washington: February 1989), p. 618.
87. United Nations High Commission on Refugees figures, February 1990, cited in *Boletín Informativo*, February 1990.
88. Jeffrey Leonard, *Natural Resources and Economic Development* (New Brunswick: Transaction Books/International Institute for Environment and Development, 1987), pp. 99, 120.
89. JRB Associates, *Honduras: Environmental Profile* (Washington: AID, 1982).
90. Manuel Torres Calderon, "Forests Going, Deserts Coming," *Latin America News Update*, August 1989.
91. David Pickles, "Honduran Forestry Lumbers into Crisis," *Financial Times*, 28 April 1989.
92. Jim Barborak, "Tough Times Ahead for Honduras" (Centro Agronómico Tropical de Investigación y Enseñanza-CATIE, undated draft).
93. Pickles, op. cit.
94. Kathleen Krog, "Reagan's Chosen Turn from Exploits to Exploitation," *Miami Herald*, 26 June 1989; *Central America Report*, 16 June 1989.
95. Denise Stanley, "Contras Contribute to Ecological Destruction in Honduras," *Earth Island Journal*, Summer 1989.
96. "U.S. Buying Chainsaws for Contras in Honduras," *Not Man Apart*, June-September 1989.

97. UPI, Tegucigalpa, 10 May 1986.

98. Hearings before a subcommittee of House Committee on Appropriations, *Foreign Operations, Export Financing, and Related Appropriations for 1989*, House of Representatives, 2nd Session, 1988.

99. *Washington Post*, 5 April 1986.

100. Leonard, op. cit., pp. 16, 18.

101. Ibid., pp. 146, 149.

102. Ibid., p. 149.

103. *Hondupress*, 5 October 1981.

104. Leonard, op. cit., p. 99.

105. Ibid., p. 90.

106. United Nations, "Estimates and Projections of Urban, Rural, and City Populations, 1950-2025," Department of International Economic and Social Affairs, 1985.

107. *Hondupress*, 28 September 1989.

108. Ibid., p. 135.

109. *Hondupress*, 17 October 1989.

110. *Central America Report*, 19 January 1990.

111. Bill Weinberg, "War on the Land: The Politics of Ecology and the Ecology of Politics in Central America," unpublished manuscript.

112. Ibid.; *Cultural Survival Quarterly*, Vol. 11 No. 3, 1987, pp. 38-45.

113. For an inventory of Honduran parks and reserves, proposed and actual, see: Gustavo Cruz, *Guía de los Parques Nacionales* (Tegucigalpa: Honduran Association for Ecology, 1986).

Chapter Five

1. Robert E. Sanchez, "Honduras: U.S. Foreign Assistance Facts," A Congressional Research Service Brief, 20 May 1988.

2. Military assistance rose from $2.3 million in fiscal year 1979 to $3.9 million in 1980, and economic assistance increased from $29.1 million to $53.1 million.

3. Richard Lapper and James Painter, *Honduras: State for Sale* (London: Latin American Bureau, 1985), p. 78.

4. Philip L. Shepherd, "The Case of the Invisible Aid," *NACLA Report on the Americas*, January-February 1988, p. 33. Philip Shepherd, "Honduras," in Morris J. Blachman, William M. LeoGrande, and Kenneth E. Sharpe, *Confronting Revolution: Security through Diplomacy in Central America* (New York: Pantheon, 1986).

5. AID-Honduras, "Briefing Book" (Tegucigalpa: January 1988).

6. For discussion of Honduran nationalism see: David Ronfeldt, *U.S. Involvement in Central America: Three Views from Honduras* (RAND Corporation, July 1989).

7. During the early 1980s COHEP resisted the complete implementation of AID's neoliberal remedies and AID directed most of its private-sector support assistance through a new breed of export-oriented business associations, most of which were created by AID. But AID never broke the hegemony of COHEP, and there was a realignment between AID and COHEP that opened the way for AID funding of COHEP beginning in 1988. For more background see: Tom Barry, *Rain of Dollars* (Albuquerque: The Resource Center, 1986), and Benjamin Crosby, "Crisis y Fragmentación: Relaciones entre los Sectores Público-Privado en Centroamérica" (Latin American and Caribbean Center, Florida International University, May 1985).

8. U.S. Embassy, *Foreign Economic Trends and Their Implications for the United States* (Washington: U.S. Department of Commerce, June 1989).

9. Ibid.

10. U.S. Department of Commerce, "Business Fact Sheets: Honduras," June 1989.

11. Resource Center Compilation of Corporations (Albuquerque: The Resource Center, 1986).

12. Ibid.

13. *Tiempo*, 6 and 27 December 1984.

14. *Hondupress*, 11 April 1989.

15. *CBI Business Bulletin*, November-December 1988.

16. For a more thorough examination of AID in Honduras and Central America see: Tom Barry and Debra Preusch, *The Soft War: The Uses and Abuses of U.S. Economic Aid in Central America* (New York: Grove Press, 1988) and Philip Shepherd, "The Honduran Economic Crisis and U.S. Economic Assistance: A Critique of Reaganomics for Honduras," unpublished manuscript.

17. *Tiempo*, 11 March 1987.

18. Estimated ESF local currency expenditures for 1988 were divided into four categories: $26.3 million for Public Development Activities, $37.5 million in Private Sector Programs, $11.7 million for the Public Sector Recurrent Budget, and $6.8 million for the AID Trust Fund. Figures from AID's "FY1990 Annual Budget Submission."

19. U.S. Agency for International Development, *Honduras: Country Development Strategy Statement FY1986* (Washington: AID, May 1984), p. 5. The statement continues: "The painful and wrenching adjustments that will take place during the retrenchment will temporarily dash the hopes of many for improved living standards. Low-income rural families will see their earnings diminish to the extent that the cost of transportation, imported agricultural inputs, and consumer goods rise in relation to the prices they can obtain for their products. The urban unemployed are the most likely to give up hope and look for solutions that threaten political stability....Thus, some of our assistance must be aimed at helping the government minimize social unrest during this difficult period."

20. Planning Minister Francisco Figueroa in 1987 revealed that 50 percent of the local currency created by ESF payments went directly to the private sector and that the government did not exercise any control over these grants. *Tribuna*, 24 March 1987.

21. Crosby, op. cit.

22. Kathleen Heffernan, "Honduras," in Eva Paus, ed., *Struggle Against Dependence* (Boulder: Westview Press, 1988). As of 1985 nontraditional exports were one-quarter below the 1980 level as a percentage of total export value.

23. U.S. Agency for International Development, AID Policy Determination 71.

24. Shepherd, "The Honduran Economic Crisis," op. cit., p. v.

25. U.S. Agency for International Development, *Honduras Project Paper: Strengthening Democratic Institutions*, 1987, Project No. 522-0296.

26. U.S. Agency for International Development, *Congressional Presentation, FY1990, Annex III* (Washington: AID, 1989), p. 107.

27. Ibid., p. 72.

28. Ibid., p. 15.

29. Interview with Roberto Figueroa, U.S. Embassy, 14 February 1990.

30. David Corn, "Foreign Aid for the Right," *The Nation*, December 18, 1989.

31. Tom Barry and Debra Preusch, *AIFLD in Central America: Agents as Organizers* (Albuquerque: The Resource Center, 1990).

32. *AIFLD Report*, December 1985.

33. Article I of the 1954 agreement reads: "Each government will make or continue to make available to the other...such equipment, materials, services, or other military assistance as the government furnishing such assistance may authorize and in accordance with such terms and conditions as may be agreed." Cited in *Honduras: A U.S. Base for Intervention* (Philadelphia: NARMIC/American Friends Service Committee, March 1989), p. 1.

34. U.S. Department of Defense, "Training U.S. National Guard Engineers in Honduras: 'General Terencio Sierra'," 1986, p. 1.

35. Erick Weaver, "La Diplomacia del Banano: El Desarrollo de las Relaciones entre los Estados Unidos y Honduras," in Victor Meza, ed., *Honduras: Pieza Clave de la Política de Estados Unidos en Centro América* (Tegucigalpa: CEDOH, 1986).

36. U.S. Department of Defense, *Congressional Presentation for Security Assistance Programs FY1990* (Washington, 1989), p. 160.

37. Honduras has an overdue FMS debt from the 1970s of $9 million. Government Accounting Office, *Security Assistance: Update of Programs and Related Activities* (Washington: GAO, December 1988), p. 21.

38. U.S. Department of Defense, *Congressional Presentation*, op. cit., p. 161.

39. Between 1946 and 1986, some 3,100 Honduran officers and enlisted men received training at the U.S. Army School of Americas.

40. U.S. Department of Defense, "Training U.S. National Guard Engineers in Honduras," op. cit.

41. Government Accounting Office, *Security Assistance: Update of Programs and Related Activities* (Washington; GAO, December 1988), p. 52.

42. Ibid., p. 54.

43. Ibid., p. 59.

44. Ibid., p. 87. The 1987 figure is a DOD estimation.

45. Philip Shepherd, "El Trágico Curso y las Consequencias de la Política Norteamericana en Honduras," in Meza, *Honduras: Pieza Clave*, op. cit., p. 127. Senator James Sasser (D-TN) called the military exercises "an open back door" to fortify the Honduran military, observing that the construction activities were often unnecessary for the success of the maneuvers. "Report on Honduras," *Congressional Record*, 8 February 1984, pp. 1122-1125.

46. In 1983 the DOD formulated a "Force Modernization" plan for Honduras that called for an annual U.S. military aid commitment of $100 million for four years. U.S. Embassy, "U.S. Military Activities in Honduras" (Tegucigalpa, February 1984).

47. The $74.5 million military-assistance package included ten FE-5 fighter jets and two F-5 training aircraft. These Mach 1.1 supersonic jets are superior to any other aircraft in Central America and replace the Super Mysteres which had been the most sophisticated in the region. See: "Statement of Edward L. King before the Subcommittee on Arms Control and Scientific Affairs and Western Hemispheric Affairs," 19 May 1987.

48. U.S. Embassy, "Handbook on Honduras: Democracy, Defense, Development, Diplomacy and Drug Control" (Tegucigalpa, Fall 1988).

49. U.S. Government Accounting Office, *Honduras: U.S. Military Presence at Soto Cano Air Base* (Washington: GAO, March 1989), p. 9.

50. Joint Task Force Bravo, "Fact Sheet J-5," 1 June 1987.

51. U.S. Department of Defense, "Training U.S. National Guard Engineers in Honduras," op. cit.

52. Ibid.

53. Ibid.
54. Shepherd, "El Trágico Curso y las Consequencias," op. cit., p. 131.
55. *Honduras: A U.S. Base for Intervention*, op. cit., pp. 2-3; *Honduras: Fuerzas Armadas 1988* (Mexico: Instituto de Investigaciones Socioeconómicas de Honduras-INSEH, 1989).
56. George Black and Anne Nelson, "Mysterious Death of Father Carney," *The Nation*, 4 August 1984.
57. "Incidentes y Costo Humano de la Presencia Militar de los Estados Unidos en Honduras," *Boletín Informativo*, CEDOH, August 1989.
58. Willard F. Barber and Neale Ranning, *Internal Security and Military Power* (Columbus: Ohio State University Press, 1966), p. 127. For more information on early military/civic action programs see: Tom Barry, *Low Intensity Conflict: The New Battlefield in Central America* (Albuquerque: The Resource Center, 1986), pp. 41-45, and C.M. Simpson, *Inside the Green Berets: The Story of the U.S. Army Special Forces* (New York: Berkeley Books, 1984).
59. *National Guard Update*, January-February 1989.
60. Major Bernard Eugene Harvey, USAF, "Military Civic Action in Honduras 1982-1985: Tactical Success, Strategic Uncertainty," CLIC Papers, Army-Air Force Center for Low Intensity Conflict, October 1988. For a critical analysis of the Harvey paper, see: Eric Shultz, "Medical Counterinsurgency in Honduras," *Honduras Update*, November-December 1988.
61. Harvey, "Military Civic Action in Honduras," op. cit.
62. Ibid., p. 2.
63. Ibid.
64. Interview with Juan Sieca Fonseca, Honduran Army Public Relations Officer, March 16, 1989.
65. Interview with COPEN director, July 1987; *Proyecciones Militares*, No. 83, January 1989.
66. *Central America Report*, 4 August 1989.
67. *Central America Report*, 25 August 1989; *Honduras Update*, October 1987.
68. Jane Hunter, *Israeli Foreign Policy: South Africa and Central America* (Boston: South End Press, 1987), p. 166. Also see Milton Jamail and Margo Gutierrez, *It's No Secret: Israel's Military Involvement in Central America* (Belmont, MA: Association of Arab-American Students, 1986).
69. Hunter, *Israeli Foreign Policy*, op. cit., p. 166.
70. *Israeli Foreign Affairs*, December 1987; *Honduras Update*, June-July 1987.
71. "Israel-Contras Link Goes Back Years, According to Israeli," *San Francisco Chronicle*, 5 December 1986; Hunter, *Israeli Foreign Policy*, op. cit., p. 145.
72. Hunter, *Israeli Foreign Policy*, op. cit., p. 146.
73. Ibid., p. 147; Edy Kaufman, "The View from Jerusalem," *The Washington Quarterly*, Fall 1984.
74. Jamail and Gutierrez, *It's No Secret*, op. cit., p. 31.
75. Hunter, *Israeli Foreign Policy*, op. cit., p. 150-151.
76. Hunter, *Israeli Foreign Policy*, op. cit., p. 151.
77. *Israeli Foreign Affairs*, December 1987.
78. Ibid.
79. *Israeli Foreign Affairs*, August 1988.

Statistics

Population

Population:	4,829,000 (1988)[1]
Urban Population:	42.2% (1988)[1]
Population Density:	112 per sq. mi. (1988)[1]
Annual Growth Rate:	3.5% (1981-1988)[1]
Literacy:	56% (1988)[2]
Ethnic Composition:[3]	
Ladino:	90%
Indian:	7%
Black:	2%
Caucasian:	1%

Health

Life Expectancy at Birth:	64.6 years (1988)[4]
Infant Mortality per 1,000 Live Births:	66 (1988)[4]

Economy

GDP:	$4,107 million (1988)[1]
Per Capita GDP:	$851 (1988)[1]
Per Capita GDP Growth Rate:[1]	
1961-1980:	2.2%
1981-1985:	-2.5%
Gross Domestic Investment:[1]	
1961-1970:	9.0%
1971-1980:	6.5%
1981-1988:	-4.3%
Income Distribution (1980):[5]	
Poorest 20% of Population:	4.3%
30% Below the Mean:	12.7%
30% Above the Mean:	23.7%
Richest 20%:	59.3%
Rural Population in Absolute Poverty:	77%[6]

(Absolute poverty is the inability to afford food providing minimum nutritional requirements.)

Land Distribution:[6]
   4% of farms comprise 56% of farmland
   64% of farms comprise 9% of farmland

External Public Debt:
   1970: $143.8 million[1]
   1987: $3,405 million[1]

Trade Balance: $50 million (1988)[7]
   Debt Servicing as % of Exports: 30.4% (1986)[4]
   External Debt as % of GNP: 68.7% (1986)[4]
   Property & Income Taxes as % of Current Revenues: 23.4% (1987)[1]

Labor Force by Sector (1987):[1]
   Agriculture: 52.5%
   Manufacturing: 13.7%
   Construction: 4.4%

Unemployment: 35% (1986)[8]

Real Minimum Wage as Compared to 1980 Wages:[1]
   1978:   102.5%
   1987:   84.0%

Top Agricultural Products as % of Total Exports (1983-1987):[1]
   Bananas: 32.7%
   Coffee: 26.7%
   Beef: 2.6%

U.S. Economic Aid[9]
(millions of dollars)

	1946-1979	1980-1987	1988	1989	1990*
Development Assistance	213.8	298.4	44.9	37.7	34.4
ESF	2.4	480.5	85.0	15.0	130.0
PL480	37.8	98.4	20.3	21.2	17.7
Peace Corps	17.0	29.2	6.5	6.3	6.2
Total	271.0	906.5	156.7	80.2	188.3

U.S. Military Aid[9]
(millions of dollars)

	1946-1979	1980-1987	1988	1989	1990*
MAP	5.6	312.4	40.0	40.0	0
FMS	12.5	39.9	0	0	20.2
IMET	8.4	7.4	1.2	1.1	1.1
Total	26.5	359.7	41.2	41.1	21.2

* Estimated

Sources:
1) Economic and Social Progress in Latin America: 1989 Report, Inter-American Development Bank; 2) World Factbook 1988, CIA; 3) Encyclopedia of the Third World, 1987; 4) Congressional Presentation Fiscal Year 1990, Annex III, Latin America and the Caribbean,

Agency for International Development; 5) CEPAL Review, April 1984; 6) Roots of Rebellion: Land and Hunger in Central America, Resource Center, 1987; 7) Notas Sobre la Economía y el Desarrollo, CEPAL, December 1988; 8) Europa Yearbook 1988; 9) U.S. Overseas Loans and Grants: Obligations and Loan Authorizations July 1, 1945-September 30, 1983, Agency for International Development, Office of Planning and Budgeting; U.S. Overseas Loans and Grants: Obligations and Loan Authorizations July 1, 1945-September 30, 1987, Agency for International Development, Office of Planning and Budgeting; Fiscal Year 1990 Summary Tables, Agency for International Development, Pat Sommers, AID, February 3, 1990.

Chronology

1502   Christopher Columbus lands on northern coast of Honduras.

1821   Honduras declares its independence from Spain as part of the Central American Federation.

1839   Honduras becomes independent republic.

1848   New constitution promulgated.

1855   Liberals removed from power.

1865   New constitution promulgated.

1876   Liberals regain power under Marco Aurelio Soto.

1880   New constitution promulgated.
        Tegucigalpa named national capital.

1891   Conservatives elected to power.

1894   New constitution promulgated.

1896   U.S. troops land in Honduras.

1899   The first banana concession is granted to the Vaccaro brothers, later to become Standard Fruit Company.

1905   U.S. troops land in Honduras for the first of five times during the next 20 years.

1907   Policarpio Bonilla overthrown and replaced by Dávila.
        U.S. banana merchant Sam Zemurray forms the Cuyamel Fruit Company.

1910   Dávila deposed by U.S. mercenaries and replaced by Manuel Bonilla.

1912   Trujillo Railroad Company wins contract to build a railway, beginning United Fruit Company's involvement in Honduras.

1921   First Congress of Workers convenes and organizes Honduras Workers Federation.

1923   Presidential elections won by General Tiburcio Carías Andino, who is prevented from taking office.

1924   Carías' forces take Tegucigalpa; new elections won by Paz Baraona.

1925   New constitution promulgated.

1926   Formation of the Federation of Workers Societies of the North.

1929   United Fruit purchases Cuyamel for $32 million.
        Formation of the Honduran Syndical Organization.

1932   Carías begins 16-year dictatorship.

1936   New constitution promulgated.

1948   Carías steps down; Nationalist Party Juan Manuel Gálvez elected president.

1952   Foundation of the Francisco Morazán military college.

1954   Elections won by Ramón Villeda Morales of Liberal Party; Vice President Julio Lozano Díaz seizes power.

Successful strike by banana workers leads to widespread organizing among other workers.

Communist Party reorganized.

1955   United Fruit workers form the Union of Tela Railroad Company Workers.

1956   Constituent elections overturned by coup; military junta led by Roque J. Rodríguez assumes power.

1957   Villeda Morales elected president; new constitution promulgated; new labor codes and social security law adopted.

1959   Abortive military coup.

1960   Resolution of Atlantic coast border dispute with Nicaragua.

1961   Introduction of agrarian-reform program.

1963   Shortly before finishing his term, Villeda is ousted by army coup led by Colonel Osvaldo López Arellano.

1965   New constitution promulgated.

Peasant leader Lorenzo Zelaya killed.

1969   "Soccer War" with El Salvador over mistreatment of Salvadorans in Honduras and related issues lasts four days.

1971   Ramón Ernesto Cruz elected president.

Pact of National Unity divides congressional seats evenly between National and Liberal Parties.

1972   Cruz deposed; López returns to power.

United States recognizes Honduran control of Swan Islands.

1974   Hurricane Fifi leaves 12,000 dead and 150,000 homeless.

1975   "Bananagate" scandal: United Brands pays a "high government official" a $1.25 million bribe for a reduction in banana taxes and saves $7.5 million.

López is overthrown and Juan Alberto Melgar Castro takes power.

Army and local landowners kill 15 peasant demonstrators, including two priests.

1976   Border conflicts with El Salvador; OAS intervenes.

1977   Las Isletas banana cooperative destroyed by soldiers who arrive in Standard Fruit's railroad cars.

1978   Melgar ousted after drug-related allegations surface; General Policarpio Paz García assumes power.

1979   President Carter strengthens ties to Honduras after the fall of Somoza in Nicaragua.

1980   Constituent Assembly elections.

"Soccer War" officially ends with signing of treaty with El Salvador.

1981   Liberal Party candidate Roberto Suazo Córdova elected president, the first civilian president in more than two decades. General Gustavo Alvarez retains power as chief of staff.

John Dimitri Negroponte becomes U.S. ambassador.

First U.S. military advisors arrive in Honduras; joint U.S.-Honduran naval and air maneuvers.

1982   Alvarez instigates change to constitution which reduces presidential authority; Constituent Assembly approves Honduras' sixteenth constitution.

Foreign Ministers of Honduras, Costa Rica, and El Salvador form the Central American Democratic Community.

Feb.   Reagan Administration pledges a 50 percent increase in military aid to Honduras. Four clandestine cemeteries discovered.

April   Strikes and land occupations are "subversive acts" in new decree.

June   Honduran army participates in joint operations with the Salvadoran army against the FMLN guerrillas.

July   Joint U.S.-Honduran military maneuvers along Nicaraguan border.

Aug.   Honduras armed forces on full alert after border clashes with Nicaragua. Strike of 30,000 teachers.

Nov.   *Newsweek* reveals that Negroponte in control of contra operations against Nicaragua.

1983   U.S. training base opens at Puerto Castilla.

Joint U.S.-Honduran Big Pine I and II military and naval maneuvers begin.

Contadora group meets for first time to develop dialogue and negotiation in Central America; parties to the peace accords include Costa Rica, El Salvador, Guatemala, Honduras, and Nicaragua.

1984   Alvarez ousted by younger officers and goes into exile; General Walter López Reyes named commander in chief of the armed forces.

Grenadier I joint military exercises along Salvadoran border with U.S., Honduran, and Salvadoran troops.

60,000 demonstrators in Tegucigalpa and 40,000 in San Pedro Sula protest U.S. presence in Honduras.

Honduran government halts U.S. training of Salvadoran soldiers at Puerto Castilla.

Army published report on human rights violations which blames left and rightwing non-Hondurans.

Kissinger Commission recommends $8 billion developmental aid to Central America and increased military assistance to Honduras, El Salvador, and Guatemala.

U.S. military aid has increased by 20 times since 1980.

Nicaragua agrees to sign Contadora treaty, but Costa Rica, El Salvador, and Honduras refuse to sign.

1985   Liberal Party candidate José Azcona Hoyo declared winner of presidential elections although National Party candidate gains most votes.

Constitutional crisis over appointment of judges.

Nicaraguan contras linked to 200 death squad killings in Honduras.

MISURA contra leader Steadman Fagoth is expelled.

Formation of the National Congress of Rural Workers (CNTC).

Big Pine III, Universal Trek '85, and Cabañas '85 joint military exercises.

Honduran army enters Colomoncagua refugee camp, killing two Salvadoran refugees and taking away ten others.

1986   López Reyes resigns and is replaced by Regalado Hernández.

Blazing Trail joint exercises.

Third revised Contadora treaty presented, Costa Rica, El Salvador, and Honduras refuse to sign.

1987   Mass repatriation of refugees from the Mesa Grande camps in Honduras.

Feb.   Costa Rica President Arias takes leadership role in regional peace initiatives, meets with representatives from El Salvador, Guatemala and Honduras in Esquipulas, Guatemala.

Aug.   Presidents of Costa Rica, El Salvador, Guatemala, Honduras, and Nicaragua sign Esquipulas II Peace Accords.

1988   Honduras requests a UN peacekeeping force to patrol its borders with El Salvador and Nicaragua.

Mar.   Arias accuses countries of El Salvador, Guatemala, Honduras, and Nicaragua with not complying fully with the Esquipulas Accords, and criticizes the presence of U.S. troops in Honduras.

1989   Esquipulas peace talks held in El Salvador after four postponements.

Sources for the chronology include: The Central America Fact Book by Tom Barry and Debra Preusch (New York: Grove Press, 1986); Conflict in Central America (United Kingdom: Longman Group Limited, 1987); Encyclopedia of the Third World (New york: Facts on File, 1987); Crisis in Central America: Regional Dynamics and U.S. Policy in the 1980s (Boulder: Westview Press, 1988); Labor Organizations in Latin America, Gerald Greenfield and Sheldon Maran, eds. (New York: Greenwood Press, 1987); Honduras: State for Sale by Richard Lapper and James Painter (London: Latin American Bureau, 1985).

Bibliography

The following periodicals are useful sources of information and analysis on Honduras:

Boletín Informativo, Centro de Documentación de Honduras (Tegucigalpa), monthly, Spanish.

Hondupress, Honduran Press Agency (Boulder and Managua), biweekly, English.

NACLA Report on the Americas, North American Congress on Latin America, bi-monthly, English.

Pensamiento Propio, Coordinadora Regional de Investigaciones Económicas y Sociales (Managua), monthly, Spanish.

The following books contain valuable background on many issues important to understanding Honduras:

Alison Acker, *Honduras: The Making of a Banana Republic* (Boston: South End Press, 1988).

Morris J. Blachman, William M. LeoGrande, and Kenneth Sharpe, *Confronting Revolution: Security Through Diplomacy in Central America* (New York: Pantheon Books, 1986).

Richard Lapper and James Painter, *Honduras: State for Sale* (London: Latin American Bureau, 1985).

James A. Morris, *Honduras: Caudillo Politics amnd Military Rulers* (Boulder: Westview Press, 1984).

Margarita Oseguera de Ochoa, *Honduras Hoy: Sociedad y Crisis Regional* (Tegucigalpa: CEDOH/CRIES, 1987).

Nancy Peckenham and Annie Street, eds., *Honduras: Portrait of a Captive Nation* (New York: Praeger Publishers, 1985).

Mark B. Rosenberg and Philip L. Shepherd, eds., *Honduras Contronts its Future: Contending Perspectives on Critical Issues* (Boulder: Lynne Rienner Publishers Inc., 1986).

For More Information

Resources

Centro de Documentación de Honduras (CEDOH)/Boletín Informativo
Apartado Postal 1882
Tegucigalpa, Honduras

Hondupress
P.O. Box 18045
Boulder, CO 80308
Apartado Postal RP-13
Managua 3, Nicaragua

Human Rights

Americas Watch
1522 K Street NW, Suite 910
Washington DC 20005

Amnesty International
322 8th Avenue
New York, NY 10001

Comité para la Defensa de los Derechos Humanos (CODEH)
Apartado Postal 1256
Tegucigalpa, Honduras

Comité de Familiares de Desaparecidos en Honduras (COFADEH)
Apartado Postal 1243
Tegucigalpa, Honduras

National Central America Health Rights Network (NCAHRN)/Links
P.O. Box 202
New York, NY 10276

Tours

Global Exchange
2141 Mission Street, Room 202
San Francisco, CA 94110

Official

Embassy of Honduras
4301 Connecticut Avenue NW
Washington DC 20008-2384

Embassy of the United States in Honduras
APO Miami, FL 34022

U.S. State Department
Citizen's Emergency Center/Travel Information
Main State Building
Washington DC 20520
(202) 647-5225

Also available from the Resource Center

The Soft War: The Uses and Abuses of U.S. Economic Aid in Central America (1988) studies the many U.S. government agencies involved in pacification, stabilization, nation-building, and low-intensity conflict programs in the region.

$14.95

Roots of Rebellion (1987) looks behind the news flashes of earthquakes and coups to the real crisis in Central America: land and hunger.

$9.00

Central America Inside Out: (forthcoming from Grove Weidenfield) includes *all* of the information you need about Central America in one handy, well-organized book!

Send your order with 15% postage & handling:
(Foreign orders: 30% postage & handling, U.S. dollars drawn on U.S. banks)

The Resource Center
Box 4506 * Albuquerque, New Mexico * 87196

--please request a free catalogue of publications--